WORKBOOK
to accompany
HORNGREN'S ACCOUNTING

11th Canadian Edition
Volume 1

Tracie L. Miller-Nobles
Austin Community College

Brenda Mattison
Tri-County Technical College

Ella Mae Matsumura
University of Wisconsin—Madison

Carol A. Meissner
Georgian College

Jo-Ann L. Johnston
British Columbia Institute of Technology

Peter R. Norwood
Langara College

 Pearson

Pearson Canada Inc., 26 Prince Andrew Place, North York, Ontario M3C 2H4.

ISBN 978-0-13-579242-1

Contents

Preface

Faculty

Welcome to Pearson's Workbook for *Horngren's Accounting*, 11th Canadian Edition. This Workbook not only supports in-class work, but is also one of the many tools that Pearson has published to support various teaching strategies.

The Workbook facilitates the flipped classroom approach to course delivery, where you might spend a portion of class time having students work either individually or in groups on guided problems. If a fully flipped class isn't your goal, but you still want to give students time in class to work on guided problem-solving exercises, this tool can be used to achieve that as well.

Students

Here is another tool to add to your toolkit for success. Read the full eText and practise some questions online. Then in the classroom, get a near-to-real-world experience of using pencil and paper to prepare for tests.

Remember, the key to success in learning any new task is practise, practise, practise. The Workbook will help you do this more efficiently because the questions are shown right where you work on the answers. It also keeps your work all neat and organized because the working papers are already formatted and ordered for you.

Pearson's Workbook: A Key for Success in School and at Work

Regardless of the course you're taking—whether you are in general business, marketing, entrepreneurship, accounting, human resources, or any other program—you will want to leave with skills that can help you get the job you want. Some of these skills will be specific to your course of study or major. These are basic skills your employers will want you to have. An accountant, for example, will be expected to know how to read a balance sheet and write journal entries. However, there are other skills essential to your success in the workplace that might not seem so obvious but are important enough that some governments call them "essential" employability skills. The Conference Board of Canada goes even further, calling them "the skills you need to enter, stay in, and progress in the world of work—whether you work on your own or as a part of a team." (http://www.conferenceboard.ca/topics/education/learning-tools/employability-skills.aspx) This Pearson Workbook was designed to help you develop these skills.

What Are Essential Employability Skills?

Essential employability skills can be grouped into six broad categories: communication, numeracy, critical thinking & problem solving, information management, interpersonal, and personal. Provincial governments think that these skills are so important that they expect everyone who graduates with a certificate or diploma to have them. Many of these skills are also referred to as "soft skills," or "21st-century skills," and represent areas like writing that are not specific to the core content of any one course but are important to your success in *all* courses, and in the working world. Being able to show prospective employers that you have these skills can make a huge difference in your ability to get the job that you want.

Pearson's Workbook is designed with the needs of college students in mind, including the need to develop and demonstrate these essential employability skills. Here's how.

COMMUNICATION SKILLS

Defining skill areas: reading, writing, speaking, listening, presenting, and visual literacy

One of the reasons why students don't develop their reading skills is simply because they have not bought their textbooks at all. Pearson eTexts and Workbooks are available at a price that will encourage as many students as possible to buy—and practise working with—their course materials. Workbooks often include short answer questions or writing activities that provide opportunities for students to practise and develop their written communication skills.

NUMERACY SKILLS

Defining skill areas: understanding and applying mathematical concepts and reasoning, analyzing and using mathematical data, and conceptualizing

Workbooks in disciplines such as accounting require students to understand and apply some mathematical concepts when answering practice questions. The spiral-bound workbook format encourages their use as in-class activity workbooks, where faculty can provide instructional support to students as they work through these problems.

CRITICAL THINKING & PROBLEM SOLVING SKILLS

Defining skill areas: analyzing, synthesizing, evaluating, decision making, and creative and innovative thinking

The exercises found in *Horngren's Accounting* are not simply factual, recall, or "skill and drill" type activities. They are created to engage students at many different levels of Bloom's Taxonomy to help develop their critical thinking and problem solving skills.

INFORMATION MANAGEMENT SKILLS

Defining skill areas: gathering and managing information, selecting and using appropriate tools and technology for a task or project, computer literacy, and internet skills

Not all of the exercises in *Horngren's Accounting* are pencil and paper activities. Some also require students to engage with applications such as Microsoft Excel, or to explain how they would utilize these tools to find the solution to a problem.

INTERPERSONAL SKILLS

Defining skill areas: teamwork, relationship management, conflict resolution, leadership, and networking

Because workbooks can be used in class, they facilitate group work and collaborative problem solving. Activities that, in the past, would have been assigned as homework to be done individually can now be implemented in ways that help students develop their interpersonal skills.

PERSONAL SKILLS

Defining skill areas: managing self, managing change and being flexible and adaptable, engaging in reflexive practice, and demonstrating personal responsibility

Making the decision to purchase course materials and actively engage with course content is one of the first steps towards demonstrating a degree of personal responsibility for success in school. The page layout of a workbook also encourages note-taking and supports the development of good study skills.

Questions by Learning Objective

Items in bold are the Serial Exercise. Students can complete them even if the previous ones were not completed.

Chapter	Learning Objective	Starters	Exercises	Problems
1	1	S1-3		
	2		E1-2	
	3	S1-5	E1-3	
	4		E1-4, E1-5, E1-7, E1-8	P1-2A
	5	S1-12, S1-13, S1-14	E1-10, E1-14, E1-15, E1-16, **E1-18**, E1-19	P1-5A, P1-7A, P1-8A
2	1	S2-1, S2-3		
	2	S2-5	E2-3, E2-5, E2-6	
	3	S2-7, S2-8	E2-7, E2-9, E2-10	P2-3A
	4	S2-10, S2-11, S2-12	E2-13, E2-15	P2-4A
	5	S2-14, S2-15	E2-19, **E2-22**	P2-5A, P2-6A, P2-7A
3	1		E? 1	
	2	S3-4		
	3	S3-8, S3-9, S3-10, S3-11, S3-12, S3-13, S3-14, S3-15, S3-16	E3-5, E3-8, E3-9, E3-10	P3-3A, P3-4A
	4		E3-14, **E3-20**	
	5		E3-15	P3-6A, P3-7A
	6	S3-19		
	A1	S3-20		
	A2	S3-21		
4	1	S4-1, S4-3, S4-4	E4-2, **E4-19**	P4-1A
	2	S4-5		
	3		E4-4, E4-5, E4-9	
	4	S4-14	E4-12	
	5	S4-16	**E4-20**	
	6	S4-19		P4-6A, P4-7A
	7	S4-21		
	A1		E4-17	

Continued

Chapter	Learning Objective	Starters	Exercises	Problems
5	1	S5-1		
	2	S5-7, S5-8, S5-9, S5-10	E5-3, E5-4, E5-6, E5-8	P5-2A, P5-3A
	3	S5-11	E5-11, **E5-25**	
	4	S5-13, S5-14	E5-14	P5-6A
	5			P5-5A, P5-7A
	6			
	A1		E5-17	
	A2		E5-23	
	A3			P5-12A
	A4			P5-13A
	B1			P5-14A
6	1	S6-1, S6-2	E6-2, E6-3, E6-4	P6-2A
	2		E6-7, **E6-21**	P6-4A, P6-6A
	3	S6-9	E6-11	P6 8A
	4	S6-11, S6-12	E6-14	
	5	S6-14		P6-14A
7	1			
	2	S7-3, S7-6	E7-2	
	3		E7-6, E7-7	
	4		E7-13	
	5	S7-15	E7-14, E7-15, **E7-16**	P7-4A, P7-5A, P7-6A, P7-7A
8	1	S8-3		
	2	S8-4		P8-3A
	3	S8-9	E8-8, E8-9, E8-10, **E8-25**	P8-4A, P8-5A
	4		E8-15, E8-16	
	5	S8-15	E8-18, E8-19, E8-21, E8-22	P8-9A
	6	S8-16		
9	1		E9-1	
	2	S9-7, S9-8	E9-3, E9-4, **E9-20**	P9-2A
	3	S9-9		
	4	S9-12	E9-9	P9-4A
	5	S9-15	E9-11	P9-6A
	6		E9-14, E9-15	P9-9A
	7	S9-20		
	A1			P9-10A
10	1		E10-2, E10-3	
	2	S10-6	E10-5, E10-6, E10-7, E10-8, E10-9	P10-2A
	3	S10-8, S10-11, S10-12	**E10-22**	P10-3A
	4	S10-14	E10-12, E10-14	P10-5A
	5			P10-7A
	6	S10-18	E10-16	P10-8A
	7		E10-21	
11	1	S11-3, S11-6	E11-2, E11-4, E11-5	
	2	S11-7		P11-1A
	3	S11-13, S11-14	E11-14	P11-3A
	4	S11-16, S11-17, S11-18	E11-16, E11-17, E11-18, **E11-20**	P11-4A, P11-5A
	5		E11-19	P11-9A
	6	Question 20		

Use the templates provided at the back of this Workbook to prepare report format balance sheets.

1 ACCOUNTING AND THE BUSINESS ENVIRONMENT

LEARNING OBJECTIVES

1 Define accounting, and describe the users of accounting information.
2 Compare and contrast the forms of business organizations.
3 Describe some concepts and principles of accounting.
4 Use the accounting equation to analyze business transactions.
5 Prepare financial statements.
6 Briefly explain the different accounting standards.

SOME USEFUL TEXT INFORMATION (add your own notes too)

EXHIBIT 1–15 | **Financial Statements of Hunter Environmental Consulting**

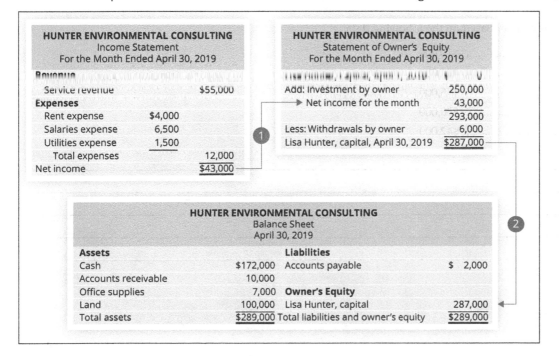

HUNTER ENVIRONMENTAL CONSULTING		
Income Statement		
For the Month Ended April 30, 2019		
Revenue		
Service revenue		$55,000
Expenses		
Rent expense	$4,000	
Salaries expense	6,500	
Utilities expense	1,500	
Total expenses		12,000
Net income		$43,000

HUNTER ENVIRONMENTAL CONSULTING	
Statement of Owner's Equity	
For the Month Ended April 30, 2019	
Lisa Hunter, capital, April 1, 2019	0
Add: Investment by owner	250,000
Net income for the month	43,000
	293,000
Less: Withdrawals by owner	6,000
Lisa Hunter, capital, April 30, 2019	$287,000

HUNTER ENVIRONMENTAL CONSULTING			
Balance Sheet			
April 30, 2019			
Assets		**Liabilities**	
Cash	$172,000	Accounts payable	$ 2,000
Accounts receivable	10,000		
Office supplies	7,000	**Owner's Equity**	
Land	100,000	Lisa Hunter, capital	287,000
Total assets	$289,000	Total liabilities and owner's equity	$289,000

S1-3 ①

For each of the users of accounting information, indicate whether they are an external decision maker (E) or an internal decision maker, (I).

a. Marketing manager _____

b. Canada Revenue Agency _____

c. Investor _____

d. Controller _____

e. Supplier _____

S1-5 ③

Match the assumption, principle, or constraint description with the appropriate term by placing a, b, c, d, e, and f on the appropriate line.

a. Cost principle of measurement _____ Benefits of the information produced by an accounting system must be greater than the costs

b. Going concern assumption _____ Amounts may be ignored if the effect on a decision maker's decision is not significant

c. Stable monetary unit assumption _____ Transactions are recorded based on the cash amount received or paid

d. Economic entity assumption _____ Ignore the effects of inflation in the accounting records

e. Cost–benefit constraint _____ Assumes that a business is going to continue operations indefinitely

f. Materiality constraint _____ A business must keep its accounting records separate from its owner's accounting records

S1-12 ⑤

Determine the expenses for September based on the following data:

September net income $10,000

Beginning owner's equity $25,000

Owner's withdrawals .... $ 5,000

Ending owner's equity $30,000

September revenue $42,000

_____
_____
_____
_____
_____

S1-13 ⑤

Picture Perfect Pet Photography specializes in taking pictures of families and their pets. Prepare the balance sheet as at January 31, 2020, using the following accounts and balances, which are currently presented in alphabetical order.

Accounts Payable .... $ 6,000

Accounts Receivable 2,000

C. Loranger, Capital 17,200

Camera Equipment 15,000

Cash 5,000

Supplies 1,200

Picture Perfect Pet Photography Balance Sheet as at January 31, 2020			
Assets	$	Liabilities	$
Cash	5 000	Accounts payable	6 000
Supplies	1 200		
Accounts receivable	2 000		
Camera Equipment	15 000		
		Owners' Equity	
		C. Loranger Capital	17 200
TOTAL ASSETS	23 200	TOTAL LIABILITIES & EQUITY.	23 200

S1-14 ⑤

Black Canary Sound Studio has just completed operations for the year ended December 31, 2019. This is the third year of operations for the company. As the owner, you want to know how well the company performed during the year. To address this question, you have assembled the data below. Use this data to prepare the income statement of Black Canary Sound Studio for the year ended December 31, 2019.

Insurance Expense	$ 3,000	Salaries Expense	$50,000
Service Revenue	150,000	Accounts Payable	8,000
Supplies Expense	1,000	Supplies	2,500
Rent Expense	18,000	Withdrawals	40,000

E1–2 ②

Indicate whether each statement below applies to a sole proprietorship, a partnership, or a corporation.

a. The life of the business is limited by the death of the owner.   _____

b. Each owner is personally liable for claims against the business.   _____

c. A business in which there is only one owner and "he or she is the business."   _____

d. Owners are not personally liable for claims against the business.   _____

e. The form of business typically used by accountants and lawyers.   _____

f. Canadian Tire and Tim Hortons are examples of this form of business.   _____

E1–3 ③

Match the situation with the best term to explain why things are done this way.

1. Every year a business uses the same account names so it can evaluate results between years.

2. When we prepare a financial statement, we show all assets at the price we paid for them.

3. A business should not spend $1,000 on counting and recounting $500 worth of inventory.

4. If we assume the business is going to go bankrupt and, as a result, we record a truck on the financial statement at the price we could get for it if we tried to sell it quickly, we are following this accounting assumption.

5. We try to include information in the accounting records such that financial statements provide enough information for readers to make an investment decision.

6. A car dealership will report profits for the parts department separate from the service department so that senior management can see how well each part of their business is doing.

a. Cost principle

b. Going concern assumption

c. Relevance characteristic

d. Cost–benefit constraint

e. Economic entity assumption

f. Comparability characteristic

E1–4 ④

Complete the following chart for the selected transactions for Martha's Muffins shown below.

a. Martha invests $10,000 cash into a business known as Martha's Muffins.

b. Martha purchases baking supplies on account for $500.

c. Martha receives and pays the kitchen's utilities bill amounting to $425.

d. Sales revenue for the current period amounts to $2,000 (all revenue transactions involved cash).

e. Martha purchases a new fridge for $3,500 cash.

	Assets	Liabilities	Owner's Equity
a)			
b)			
c)			
d)			
e)			
Totals			

E1-5 ④

Compute the missing amount in the accounting equation for each business.

Make lots of notes in the margins so you can study from them later. Here you need to remember that A = L + OE.

	Assets	=	Liabilities	+	Owner's Equity
Economy Cuts	_____		$120,000		$40,000
Marpole Dry Cleaners	$100,000		_____		$50,000
Dauphin Gift and Cards	$145,000		$115,000		_____

E1-7 ④

Indicate the effects of the following business transactions on the accounting equation of a proprietorship.

	Accounts	Account Types	Increase/Decrease
a. Received $50,000 cash from the owner.	Cash Owner, Capital	Asset Owner's Equity	Increase Increase
b. Paid the current month's office rent of $4,000.			
c. Paid $3,500 cash to purchase office supplies.			
d. Performed engineering services for a client on account, $6,000.			
e. Purchased office furniture on account at a cost of $5,000.			
f. Received cash on account, $3,000.			
g. Paid cash on account, $2,500.			
h. Sold land for $50,000 cash, which was the business's cost of the land.			
i. Performed engineering services for a client and received cash of $6,000.			

Extra Statement Paper

E1-8 ④

Gayle Hayashi, M.D., opens a medical clinic. During her first month of operation, January, the clinic, entitled Hayashi Medical Clinic, experienced the following events:

Jan.   6   Hayashi invested $250,000 in the clinic by opening a bank account in the name of Hayashi Medical Clinic.

9   Hayashi Medical Clinic paid cash for land costing $150,000. There are plans to build a clinic on the land. Until then, the business will rent an office.

12   The clinic purchased medical supplies for $10,000 on account.

15   On January 15, Hayashi Medical Clinic officially opened for business.

15–31   During the rest of the month, the clinic earned professional fees of $20,000 and received cash immediately.

15–31   The clinic paid cash expenses: employee salaries, $5,000; office rent, $4,000; utilities, $500.

28   The clinic sold supplies to another clinic at cost for $1,000.

31   The clinic paid $4,000 on the account from January 12.

Required   Analyze the effects of these events on the accounting equation of Hayashi Medical Clinic.

Analysis of Transactions

Some charts have information filled in **to save you time** so you can focus on the important parts of the questions.

| DATE | ASSETS | | | | = LIABILITIES + | | OWNER'S EQUITY | | | | |
	CASH +	MEDICAL SUPPLIES +	LAND	=	ACCOUNTS PAYABLE +	G. HAYASHI CAPITAL +	SERVICE REVENUE –	RENT EXPENSE –	SALARIES EXPENSE –	UTILITIES EXPENSE

E1-10 ④ ⑤

The accounting records of Chiang Consulting Services contain the following accounts, which you are to classify. First, indicate whether each account listed is a(n) asset (A), liability (L), owner's equity (OE), revenue (R), or expense (E) account. Then indicate whether each account listed appears on the balance sheet (B), income statement (I), statement of owner's equity (SOE), or cash flow statement (CF). Some accounts can appear on more than one statement.

	1. Type of Account	2. Statement(s)
Supplies Expense		
Accounts Receivable		
J. Chiang, Capital		
Computer Equipment		
Consulting Service Revenue		
Accounts Payable		
Rent Expense		
Cash		
J. Chiang, Withdrawals		
Supplies		
Note Payable		

Extra Statement Paper

Use the following information to answer E1–14 through E1–16.

The account balances of Wilson Towing Service at June 30, 2020, follow:

Equipment.......... *BS*	$ 25,850	Service Revenue ...... *IS*	$ 15,000
Office Supplies.... *BS*	1,000	Accounts Receivable.... *BS*	9,000
Note Payable...... *BS*	6,800	Accounts Payable...... *BS*	8,000
Rent Expense...... *IS*	900	J. Wilson, Capital, June 1, 2020 *OE*	3,250
Cash............ *B/S*	1,400	Salaries Expense ...... *IS*	2,400
J. Wilson, Withdrawals.... *OE*	3,500	✱ Investment $11 000

E1–14 ⑤

Required

1. Prepare the income statement for Wilson Towing Service for the month ending June 30, 2020. List expenses from the highest to the lowest dollar amount.

2. What does the income statement report?

Wilson Towing Service
Income Statement
for the Month ending June 30, 2020

	$	$
Revenue		
Service revenue		15 000
Expenses		
Rent expense	900	
Salaries expense	2 400	
Total expenses		(3 300)
Net Income		11 700

Income statement reports the total revenues earned and total expenses incurred in the day to day running of a business.

E1–15 ⑤

Required

1. Prepare the statement of owner's equity for Wilson Towing Service for the month ending June 30, 2020. Assume Wilson invested $11,000 during June.

2. What does the statement of owner's equity report?

	$
Wilson Towing Service	
Statement of Owner's Equity	
for the month ended June 30, 2020	
J. Wilson Capital	$
Add: Capital as at 1st June 2020	3 250
Net Income for the month.	11 700
(+) Investment 11000 →	25 950
Less: J. Wilson Withdrawals.	(3 500)
	22 450

Statement of Owner's equity shows the financial position of the owner.

(+) Investment # 11 000 was not printed.

E1–16 ⑤

Required

1. Prepare the balance sheet for Wilson Towing Service as of June 30, 2020.

2. What does the balance sheet report?

Wilson Towing Service			
Balance sheet			
as at June 30, 2020			
Assets	$	Liabilities	$
		Accounts payable	8 000
Cash	1 400	Note payable	6 800
Accounts receivable	9 000		
Office supplies	1 000		
Equipment	25 850		
		Owners' Equity	
		J. Wilson Capital	22 450
TOTAL ASSETS	37 250	TOTAL LIABILITIES & EQUITY	37 250

Balance sheet is measure of financial strength of the business.

E1-18 ③ ④ ⑤ Serial Exercise

The Serial Exercise involves a company that will be revisited throughout relevant chapters in Volume 1 and Volume 2. You can complete the Serial Exercises using MyLab Accounting.

Look for Canyon Canoe Company in each chapter. This Serial Exercise question follows the same company throughout the text.

Canyon Canoe Company is a company that rents canoes for use on local lakes and rivers. Amber Wilson graduated from university about 10 years ago. She worked for a large accounting firm and became a CPA. Because she loves the outdoors, she decided to begin a new business that will combine her love of outdoor activities with her business knowledge. Amber decides that she will create a new sole proprietorship, Canyon Canoe Company. The business began operations on November 1, 2020.

Nov.	1	Amber Wilson invested $16,000 cash in the business by opening a bank account in the name of Canyon Canoe Company.
	2	The company leased a building and paid $1,200 for the first month's rent.
	3	The company purchased canoes for $4,800 on account.
	4	The company purchased office supplies on account, $750.
	7	The company earned $1,400 cash for the rental of canoes.
	13	The company paid $1,500 cash for salaries.
	15	Amber Wilson withdrew $50 cash from the business for personal use.
	16	The company received a bill for $150 for utilities, which will be paid later.
	20	The company received a bill for $175 for cellphone expenses. The bill will be paid later.
	22	The company rented canoes to Early Start Daycare on account, $3,000.
	26	Canyon Canoe Company paid $1,000 of the amount owed for the November 3 purchase that was made on account.
	28	The company received $750 from Early Start Daycare as partial payment for the canoe rental on November 22.
	30	Amber Wilson withdrew $100 cash from the business for personal use.

Required

1. Analyze the effects of Canyon Canoe Company's transactions on the accounting equation. Use the format of Exhibit 1–11, Panel B on page 19 in your text, and include these headings: Cash; Accounts Receivable; Office Supplies; Canoes; Accounts Payable; Amber Wilson, Capital; Amber Wilson, Withdrawals; Canoe Rental Revenue; Rent Expense; Salaries Expense; Utilities Expense; and Telephone Expense.

2. Prepare the income statement of Canyon Canoe Company for the month ended November 30, 2020. List expenses in this order: Rent Expense; Salaries Expense; Utilities Expense; and Telephone Expense.

3. Prepare the statement of owner's equity for the month ended November 30, 2020.

4. Prepare the balance sheet as of November 30, 2020.

Analysis of Transactions

DATE	ASSETS				= LIABILITIES +	OWNER'S EQUITY							
	CASH +	ACCTS REC. +	OFFICE SUPPLIES +	CANOES =	ACCOUNTS PAYABLE =	AMBER WILSON, CAPITAL +	AMBER WILSON, WITHDRAWALS –	CANOE RENTAL REVENUE +	RENT EXPENSE –	SALARIES EXPENSE –	UTILITIES EXPENSE –	TELEPHONE EXPENSE

TOTAL ASSETS = $ _____   TOTAL LIABILITIES AND OWNER'S EQUITY = $ _____

Extra Statement Paper

E1–19 ④ ⑤

Compute the missing amounts for each of the following businesses:

	Fraser Co.	Delta Co.	Pine Co.
Beginning:			
Assets...	$350,000	$300,000	$540,000
Liabilities...	200,000	120,000	360,000
Ending:			
Assets...	$500,000	$360,000	$ _____
Liabilities...	250,000	160,000	480,000
Owner's equity:			
Investments by owner.............................	$ _____	$ 0	$ 50,000
Withdrawals by owner.............................	250,000	150,000	220,000
Income Statement:			
Revenues...	$660,000	$350,000	$900,000
Expenses...	460,000	$ _____	675,000

Calculations:

P1-2A ③ ④

Jon Conlin, CPA, was an accountant and partner in a large firm. Recently, he resigned his position to open his own accounting business, which he operates as a proprietorship.

The following events took place during the organizing phase of his new business and its first month of operations:

Jul.	4	Conlin received $100,000 cash from his former partners in the firm from which he resigned.
	5	Conlin invested $50,000 cash in his business.
	5	The business paid office rent expense for the month of July, $3,000.
	6	The business paid $1,000 cash for letterhead stationery for the office.
	7	The business purchased office furniture on account for $7,000, promising to pay within six months.
	10	Conlin sold 2,000 shares of Royal Bank stock, which he had owned for several years, receiving $25,000 cash from his stockbroker.
	11	Conlin deposited the $25,000 cash from sale of the Royal Bank shares in his personal bank account.
	12	A representative of a large construction company telephoned Conlin and told him of the company's intention to transfer its accounting work to Conlin's business.
	29	The business performed an audit for a client and submitted the bill for services, $10,000. The business expected to collect from this client within two weeks.
	31	Conlin withdrew $3,000 cash from the business.

Required

1. Classify each of the preceding events as one of the following (insert a b or c next to the appropriate date below):

   a. A business transaction to be accounted for by the business.

   b. A business-related event but not a transaction to be accounted for by the business at this time.

   c. A personal transaction not to be accounted for by the business.

2. Analyze the effects of the above events on the accounting equation of the business. Use a format similar to Exhibit 1–11, Panel B, on page 19 in your text.

Requirement 1

CLASSIFICATION OF TRANSACTIONS

July 4 _____	July 10 _____
5 _____	11 _____
5 _____	12 _____
6 _____	29 _____
7 _____	31 _____

Requirement 2

Analysis of Transactions

DATE	ASSETS				= LIABILITIES	+	OWNER'S EQUITY			
	CASH	+ ACCOUNTS RECEIVABLE	+ OFFICE SUPPLIES	+ FURNITURE	= ACCOUNTS PAYABLE	+ J. CONLIN, CAPITAL	− J. CONLIN, WITHDRAWAL	+ SERVICE REVENUE	− RENT EXPENSE

19

P1–5A ④ ⑤

Presented below are the amounts of the assets and liabilities of Canadian Gardening Consultants as of December 31, 2020, and the revenues and expenses of the company for the year ended December 31, 2020. The items are listed in alphabetical order.

Accounts Payable	$ 57,000	Insurance Expense	$ 4,500
Accounts Receivable	36,000	Interest Expense	15,000
Advertising Expense	48,500	Land	37,500
		J. Wu, Withdrawals	$103,500
Building	300,000	Note Payable	195,000
Cash	15,000	Salaries Expense	240,000
Computer Equipment	165,000	Salaries Payable	22,500
Courier Expense	7,000	Service Revenue	450,000
Furniture	45,000	Supplies	7,500

The opening balance of owner's equity was $300,000. During the year the owner made no investments.

Required

1. Prepare the business's income statement for the year ended December 31, 2020. List expenses in order from highest to lowest amount.
2. Prepare the statement of owner's equity of the business for the year ended December 31, 2020.
3. Prepare the balance sheet of the business at December 31, 2020.
4. Answer these questions about the business:
   a. Was the result of operations for the year a profit or a loss? How much was it?
   b. Did the business's owner's equity increase or decrease during the year? How would this affect the business's ability to borrow money from a bank in the future?
   c. How much in total economic resources does the business have at December 31, 2020, as it moves into the new year? How much does the business owe? What is the dollar amount of the owner's portion of the business at December 31, 2020?

Requirement 1

Requirement 2

Requirement 3

Requirements 4 a. – c.

P1–7A ④ ⑤

Mary Reaney is the proprietor of a career counselling and employee search business, Reaney Personnel Services. The following amounts summarize the financial position of the business on August 31, 2020:

	Cash	+	Accounts Receivable	+	Office Supplies	+	Furniture	=	Accounts Payable	+	M. Reaney, Capital
					Assets			**=**	**Liabilities**	**+**	**Owner's Equity**
Bal.	40,000		35,000				95,000		55,000		115,000

During September 2020 the following company transactions occurred:

a. Reaney deposited $80,000 cash in the business bank account.

b. Performed services for a client and received cash of $5,000.

c. Paid off the August 31 balance of accounts payable.

d. Purchased supplies on account, $6,000.

e. Collected cash from a customer on account, $7,500.

f. Consulted on a large downsizing by a major corporation and billed the client for services rendered, $48,000.

g. Recorded the following business expenses for the month:
    (1) Paid co-op student for salaries—$5,000.
    (2) Paid advertising—$3,000.

h. Purchased office supplies at an auction for $1,000 cash.

i. Reaney withdrew $8,000 cash.

Required

1. Analyze the effects of the above transactions on the accounting equation of Reaney Personnel Services. Adapt the format of Exhibit 1–11, Panel B, on page 19 in your text. Add additional columns to the chart as needed.

2. Prepare the income statement of Reaney Personnel Services for the month ended September 30, 2020. List expenses in decreasing order of amount.

3. Prepare the business's statement of owner's equity for the month ended September 30, 2020.

4. Prepare the balance sheet of Reaney Personnel Services at September 30, 2020.

Requirement 1

Analysis of Transactions

DATE	ASSETS				= LIABILITIES +	OWNER'S EQUITY					
	CASH	+ ACCOUNTS RECEIVABLE	+ OFFICE SUPPLIES	+ FURNITURE	= ACCOUNTS PAYABLE	+ M. REANEY CAPITAL	− M. REANEY WITHDRAWALS	+ SERVICE REVENUE	− ADVERT. EXPENSE	− SALARIES EXPENSE	

Requirement 2

Requirement 3

Requirement 4

P1–8A ④ ⑤

Terrace Board Rentals was started on January 1, 2019, by Ryan Terrace with an investment of $50,000 cash. The company rents out snowboards and related gear from a small store. During the first 11 months, Terrace made additional investments of $20,000 and borrowed $40,000 from the bank for the business. He did not withdraw any funds. The balance sheet accounts, excluding Terrace's capital account, at November 30, 2019, are as follows:

Cash..	$45,000
Accounts Receivable..............................	15,000
Rental Gear...	32,000
Rental Snowboards	48,000
Store Equipment.....................................	30,000
Accounts Payable...................................	12,000
Note Payable...	40,000

The following transactions took place during the month of December 2019:

Dec. 1 The business paid $5,000 for the month's rent on the store space.

4 The business signed a one-year lease for the rental of additional store space at a cost of $4,000 per month. The lease is effective January 1. The business will pay the first month's rent in January.

6 Rental revenues for the week were Gear, $4,000; Boards, $10,000. Three-quarters of the fees were paid in cash and the rest on account.

10 The business paid the accounts payable from November 30, 2019.

12 The business purchased gear for $20,000 and boards for $40,000, all on account.

13 Rental revenues for the week were Gear, $7,000; Boards, $14,000. All the fees were paid in cash.

15 The company received payment for the accounts receivable owing at November 30, 2019.

18 The company purchased store equipment for $10,000 by paying $3,000 cash with the balance due in 60 days.

20 Rental revenues for the week were Gear, $8,000; Boards, $14,000. Half the fees were paid in cash and half on account.

21   Terrace withdrew $7,000.

24   The company paid the balance owing for the purchases made on December 12.

27   Rental revenues for the week were Gear, $6,000; Boards, $10,000. All the fees were paid in cash.

27   The company received payment for rental fees on account from December 6.

31   The company paid its employees for the month of December. The total salaries expense was $10,000.

31   Terrace paid the utility bill for the month of December, which was $4,000.

Required

1. What is the total net income earned by the business over the period of January 1, 2019, to November 30, 2019?

2. Analyze the effects of the December 2019 transactions on the accounting equation of Terrace Board Rentals. Include the account balances from November 30, 2019. Adapt the format of Exhibit 1–11, Panel B, on page 19 in your text.

3. Prepare the income statement for Terrace Board Rentals for the month ended December 31, 2019. List expenses in decreasing order of amount.

4. Prepare the statement of owner's equity for Terrace Board Rentals for the month ended December 31, 2019.

5. Prepare the balance sheet for Terrace Board Rentals at December 31, 2019.

6. Terrace has expressed concern that although the business seems to be profitable and growing, he constantly seems to be investing additional money into it. Prepare a reply to his concerns.

Requirement 1

Requirement 2

DATE	ASSETS					= LIABILITIES		+	OWNER'S EQUITY					
	CASH +	ACCOUNTS RECEIVABLE +	RENTAL GEAR +	RENTAL SNOWB'DS +	STORE EQUIP. =	ACCOUNTS PAYABLE +	NOTE PAYABLE +	R. TERRACE CAPITAL −	R. TERRACE WITHDRAW +	RENTAL REVENUE −	RENTAL EXPENSE −	SALARIES EXPENSE −	UTILITIES EXPENSE

Requirement 3

Requirement 4

Requirement 5

Requirement 6

Extra Statement Paper

2 RECORDING BUSINESS TRANSACTIONS

LEARNING OBJECTIVES

1 Define and use key accounting terms.
2 Apply the rules of debit and credit.
3 Analyze and record transactions in the journal.
4 Post from the journal to the ledger.
5 Prepare and use a trial balance.

SOME USEFUL TEXT INFORMATION (add your own notes too)

EXHIBIT 2–7 | Final Rules of Debit and Credit

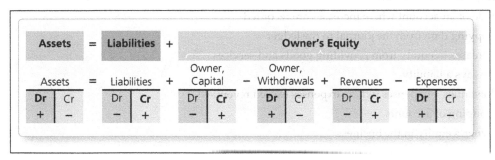

EXHIBIT 2–9 | Making a Journal Entry and Posting to the Ledger

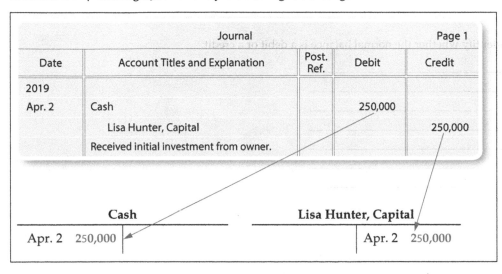

S2-1 ①

Put the steps in the accounting cycle in the proper sequence by inserting the numbers 1 to 11.

a. Prepare a post-closing trial balance ✓ _____11_____

b. Prepare an adjusted trial balance _____7_____

c. Identify and analyze the transaction _____1_____

d. Prepare the unadjusted trial balance ✓ _____4_____

e. Post adjusting journal entries to the ledger ✓ _____6_____

f. Post from the journal to the ledger accounts ✓ _____3_____

g. Journalize adjusting journal entries ✓ _____5_____

h. Journalize closing entries ✓ _____9_____

i. Prepare financial statements ✓ _____8_____

j. Post closing entries to the ledger ✓ _____10_____

k. Record transaction in a journal ✓ _____2_____

S2-3 ①

Accounting has its own vocabulary and basic relationships. Match the accounting terms at left with the corresponding definitions at right.

✓ C	1. Credit	A. Record of transactions
✗ I D	2. Normal balance	B. Always an asset
✓ G	3. Payable	C. Right side of an account
✓ A	4. Journal	D. Side of an account where increases are recorded
✗ F B	5. Receivable	E. Copying data from the journal to the ledger
✓ J	6. Capital	F. Increases in equity from providing goods and services
✓ E	7. Posting	G. Always a liability
✗ B F	8. Revenue	H. Revenues – Expenses (where expenses exceed revenues)
✓ H	9. Net loss	I. Grouping of accounts
✗ D I	10. Ledger	J. Owner's equity in the business

S2-5 ②

For each of the following accounts, identify whether the normal balance is a debit or a credit:

a. Accounts Payable _____Credit_____

b. J. Yuen, Withdrawals _____Debit_____

c. Utilities Expense _____Debit_____

d. Cash _____Debit_____

e. Service Revenue _____Credit_____

f. Rent Expense _____Debit_____

g. Accounts Receivable _____Debit_____

S2-7 ③

Jonathan Wen started a business to offer development of online stores for small businesses. Record the following transactions in the journal of the business. Include an explanation with each journal entry.

Sep. 1   Wen invested $29,000 cash in a business bank account to start his business. The business received the cash and gave Wen owner's equity in the business.

   2   Purchased computer equipment on account, $9,500.

   2   Paid cash for September's office rent of $4,100.

   3   Recorded $6,800 revenue for services rendered to clients on account.

Journal					
DATE		ACCOUNT TITLES AND EXPLANATIONS	POST REF.	DEBIT	CREDIT
Sep	1	J. Wen capital			29 000
		cash		29 000	
Sep	2	Creditor			9 500
		Computer equipment		9500	
Sep	2	office rent		4100	
		cash			4100
Sep	3	Debtor (clients)		6800	
		Service revenue			6800
		lecturer's exercise			
	①	Inventory		100 000	
		Bank loan / accounts payable			100 000
	②	Accounts payable		10 000	
		Cash			10 000
	③	Accounts receivable			50 000
		Cash		50 000	
		Bank loan		50 000	
		cash			50 000

S2–8 ③

After operating for a couple of weeks, Jonathan Wen's business completed the following transactions during the latter part of September:

Sep. 22   Performed service for clients on account, $6,000.

30   Received cash on account from clients, $4,500.

30   Received an Internet bill, $150, which will be paid during November.

30   Paid cash for advertising expense of $900.

30   Paid cash for monthly salary to his assistant, $3,900.

Journalize the business transactions. Include an explanation with each journal entry.

Journal					
DATE		ACCOUNT TITLES AND EXPLANATIONS	POST REF.	DEBIT	CREDIT
Sept	22	Account Receivable		6000	
		Service revenue			6000
		Performed Services for revenue			
Sept	30	Cash		4500	
		Accounts receivable			4500
		cash received for services			
	30	Internet expenses		150	
		Accounts payable			150
		Received internet bill			
	30	Advertising expense		900	
		Cash			900
		Payment for advertising			
	30	Salary expenses		3900	
		cash			3900
		Paid Assistants monthly salary			

S2-10 ③ ④

Nancy Carpenter Optical Dispensary bought supplies on account for $10,000 on September 8. On September 22, the company paid $4,000 on account.

1. Journalize the two transactions for Nancy Carpenter Optical Dispensary. Include an explanation for each transaction.

2. Open the Accounts Payable T-account and post to Accounts Payable. Compute the balance and denote it as *Bal*.

Requirement 1

Journal

DATE	ACCOUNT TITLES AND EXPLANATIONS	POST REF.	DEBIT	CREDIT

Requirement 2

Accounts Payable

S2-11 ③ ④

On October 5, Tina Serelio performed legal services for a client who could not pay immediately. The business expected to collect the $12,000 the following month. On November 4, the business received $5,500 cash from the client.

1. Record the two transactions for Tina Serelio, Lawyer. Include an explanation for each transaction.

2. Open these T-accounts: Cash; Accounts Receivable; Service Revenue. Post to all three accounts. Compute each account's balance and denote it as *Bal*.

3. Answer these questions based on your analysis:

    a. How much did the business earn? Which account shows this amount?

    b. How much in total assets did the business acquire as a result of the two transactions? Identify each asset and show its amount.

Requirement 1

DATE		ACCOUNT TITLES AND EXPLANATIONS	POST REF.	DEBIT	CREDIT
Oct	5th	Accounts receivable		12 000	
		Service revenue			12000
		Performed services on account			
Nov	4th	Cash		5500	
		Accounts receivable			5 500
		Received part payment from client			

Journal (table title above)

Requirement 2

Cash
Nov 4 A/R 5500
Bal 5500

Accounts Receivable
Oct 5 serv. rev. 12000 | Nov 4 Cash 5500
Bal 6500

Service Revenue
Oct 5 A/R 12000
Bal 12000

Requirement 3

(3) (a) The revenue earned is $12 000 and is shown on Service Rev account.

(b) The assets acquired are cash $5500 and A/R $6500 therefore total assets acquired by the business is $12000.

S2–12 ④

Calculate the account balance for each of the following T-accounts:

Accounts Receivable		Cash		Accounts Payable	
2,700	2,700	67,500	4,200	1,100	4,600
5,800	1,100	16,800	12,300		700
4,900	850				
	4,090				

S2–14 ④ ⑤

Use the information shown below to prepare a trial balance for Balzy Indoor Tennis Club at November 30, 2020.

Balzy Indoor Tennis Club
General Ledger

Cash	10002	Furniture	17500	Accounts Payable	20001	Stan Balzy, Capital	30001
5,000	150	5,500		3,000	9,640		27,000
12,600	800			3,000	100		
955	475						
6,200	290						

Stan Balzy, Withdrawals	30002	Sales Revenue	40001	Supplies Expense	51200	Rent Expense	53200
1,200			5,500	2,500		4,000	

	Unadjusted Trial Balance		
ACCT. NO.	ACCOUNT	DEBIT	CREDIT

S2-15 ⑤

A+ Roofers reported the following summarized data at December 31, 2020. Accounts appear in no particular order.

Revenue	$32,000	Note Payable	$17,000
Equipment	43,000	Cash	6,000
Accounts Payable	1,000	Expenses	26,000
Capital	25,000		

Prepare the unadjusted trial balance of A+ Roofers at December 31, 2020. List the accounts in proper order, as in Exhibit 2–12.

ACCOUNT	DEBIT	CREDIT

E2-3 ②

Indicate whether each account listed below is a(n) asset (A), liability (L), owner's equity (OE), revenue (R), or expense (E) account.

Salaries Payable	_____	Salaries Expense	_____
Land	_____	Rent Revenue	_____
L. Graham, Capital	_____	Computer Equipment	_____
Rent Expense	_____	Note Payable	_____
Supplies	_____	Prepaid Rent	_____
Accounts Payable	_____	L. Graham, Withdrawals	_____

E2-5 ②

Indicate whether each account listed below is a(n) asset (A), liability (L), owner's equity (OE), revenue (R), or expense (E) account. Next to each answer, indicate whether the account's normal balance is a debit (Dr) or a credit (Cr).

Accounts Payable	_____ ; _____	Cash	_____ ; _____
Service Revenue	_____ ; _____	Rent Expense	_____ ; _____
K. Lockyer, Withdrawals	_____ ; _____	Vehicles	_____ ; _____
Rent Revenue	_____ ; _____	Note Payable	_____ ; _____
Accounts Receivable	_____ ; _____	Land	_____ ; _____
Insurance Expense	_____ ; _____	K. Lockyer, Capital	_____ ; _____

E2-6 ②

a. Indicate on which side of these accounts—debit (Dr) or credit (Cr)—you would record an increase.

_____	Accounts Receivable	_____	Salaries Expense
_____	John Ladner, Capital	_____	Interest Payable
_____	Service Revenue	_____	Furniture

b. Indicate on which side of these accounts—debit (Dr) or credit (Cr)—you would record a decrease.

_____	Note Payable	_____	Land
_____	Cash	_____	Accounts Payable
_____	Income Tax Payable	_____	Income Tax Expense

E2-7 ② ③

The following transactions occurred for Anderson Moving Company:

Jul. 2   Received $10,000 contribution from Bill Anderson in exchange for capital.

4   Paid utilities expense of $400.

5   Purchased equipment on account for $2,100.

10   Performed services for a client on account, $2,000.

12   Borrowed $7,000 cash, signing a note payable.

19   The owner, Bill Anderson, withdrew $500 cash from the business.

21   Purchased office supplies for $800 and paid cash.

27   Paid the liability from July 5.

Required   Journalize the transactions of Anderson Moving Company. Include an explanation with each journal entry. Use the following accounts: Cash; Accounts Receivable; Office Supplies; Equipment; Accounts Payable; Note Payable; B. Anderson, Capital; B. Anderson, Withdrawals; Service Revenue; Utilities Expense.

Journal

DATE		ACCOUNT TITLES AND EXPLANATIONS	POST REF.	DEBIT	CREDIT

E2-9 ③

Yula's Yoga engaged in the following transactions during March 2020, its first month of operations:

Mar. 1 The business received a $15,000 cash investment from Yula Gregore to start Yula's Yoga.

1 Paid $4,000 cash to rent a yoga studio for the month of March.

4 Purchased studio supplies for $4,000 on account.

6 Presented a wellness seminar for a corporate customer and received cash, $3,000.

9 Paid $1,000 on accounts payable.

17 Taught yoga classes for customers on account, $800.

Required Record the preceding transactions in the journal of Yula's Yoga. Identify transactions by their date and include an explanation for each entry, as illustrated in the chapter. Use the following accounts: Cash; Accounts Receivable; Studio Supplies; Accounts Payable; Yula Gregore, Capital; Service Revenue; Rent Expense.

	Journal			
DATE	ACCOUNT TITLES AND EXPLANATIONS	POST REF.	DEBIT	CREDIT

E2–10 ③

Journalize the following transactions for Deresh DJ Services:

May 3   Owner, Liam Deresh, invested $2,500 cash into the business.

4   Rented a sound system and paid one month's rent, $1,100.

6   Performed DJ services on account, $1,700.

11   Paid $600 cash for equipment.

14   Owner, Liam Deresh, withdrew $500 cash for personal use.

18   Purchased $40 of supplies for cash.

| \

multicolumn{5}{c}{**Journal**} |
|---|---|---|---|---|
| DATE | ACCOUNT TITLES AND EXPLANATIONS | POST REF. | DEBIT | CREDIT |
| | | | | |
| | | | | |
| | | | | |
| | | | | |
| | | | | |
| | | | | |
| | | | | |
| | | | | |
| | | | | |
| | | | | |
| | | | | |
| | | | | |
| | | | | |
| | | | | |
| | | | | |
| | | | | |
| | | | | |
| | | | | |
| | | | | |
| | | | | |
| | | | | |
| | | | | |
| | | | | |
| | | | | |
| | | | | |
| | | | | |
| | | | | |
| | | | | |
| | | | | |
| | | | | |
| | | | | |
| | | | | |
| | | | | |

E2-13 ③ ④

On July 2, 2020, Efficient Energy Services performed an energy audit for an industrial client and earned $4,000 of revenue on account. On July 14, 2020, the company received a cheque for the entire amount.

Required

1. Journalize the two transactions on the sixth page of the journal. Include an explanation for each transaction.
2. Create the Accounts Receivable three-column ledger and post the two transactions. The account number for Accounts Receivable is 12001.

Journal

DATE		ACCOUNT TITLES AND EXPLANATIONS	POST REF.	DEBIT	CREDIT

ACCOUNT ACCOUNTS RECEIVABLE					ACCOUNT NO. 12001	
DATE		ITEM	JRNL. REF.	DEBIT	CREDIT	BALANCE

E2-15 ③ ④

Journalize the following May 2020 transactions on the ninth page of the journal, then post to the ledger accounts. Use the dates to identify the transactions.

May 2   Florence Yarrow opened a strategic consulting firm by investing $39,200 cash and office furniture valued at $16,200.

2   Paid cash for May's rent of $2,500.

2   Purchased office supplies on account, $1,800.

15   Paid employee salary, $4,000 cash.

17   Paid $1,200 of the account payable from May 2.

19   Performed consulting service on account, $69,000.

30   Withdrew $8,000 cash for personal use.

Journal					Page 9
DATE		ACCOUNT TITLES AND EXPLANATIONS	POST REF.	DEBIT	CREDIT

ACCOUNT	CASH				ACCOUNT NO. 1100
DATE	ITEM	JRNL. REF.	DEBIT	CREDIT	BALANCE

ACCOUNT	ACCOUNTS RECEIVABLE				ACCOUNT NO. 1300
DATE	ITEM	JRNL. REF.	DEBIT	CREDIT	BALANCE

ACCOUNT	OFFICE SUPPLIES				ACCOUNT NO. 1500
DATE	ITEM	JRNL. REF.	DEBIT	CREDIT	BALANCE

ACCOUNT	OFFICE FURNITURE				ACCOUNT NO. 1800
DATE	ITEM	JRNL. REF.	DEBIT	CREDIT	BALANCE

ACCOUNT	ACCOUNTS PAYABLE				ACCOUNT NO. 2100
DATE	ITEM	JRNL. REF.	DEBIT	CREDIT	BALANCE

ACCOUNT	FLORENCE YARROW, CAPITAL				ACCOUNT NO. 3100
DATE	ITEM	JRNL. REF.	DEBIT	CREDIT	BALANCE

ACCOUNT	FLORENCE YARROW, WITHDRAWALS				ACCOUNT NO. 3200
DATE	ITEM	JRNL. REF.	DEBIT	CREDIT	BALANCE

ACCOUNT	CONSULTING REVENUE				ACCOUNT NO. 4100
DATE	ITEM	JRNL. REF.	DEBIT	CREDIT	BALANCE

ACCOUNT	RENT EXPENSE				ACCOUNT NO. 5500
DATE	ITEM	JRNL. REF.	DEBIT	CREDIT	BALANCE

ACCOUNT	SALARIES EXPENSE				ACCOUNT NO. 5600
DATE	ITEM	JRNL. REF.	DEBIT	CREDIT	BALANCE

E2–19 ⑤

After recording the transactions in E2-15, prepare the unadjusted trial balance of Yarrow Strategic Consulting at May 31, 2020.

	Unadjusted Trial Balance		
ACCT. NO.	ACCOUNT	DEBIT	CREDIT

	Extra Journal Paper			
DATE	ACCOUNTS TITLES AND EXPLANATIONS	POST REF.	DEBIT	CREDIT

E2-22 ③ ④ ⑤ Serial Exercise

The Serial Exercise involves a company that will be revisited throughout relevant chapters in Volume 1 and Volume 2. You can complete the Serial Exercises using MyLab Accounting.

This exercise continues with the company introduced in Chapter 1, Canyon Canoe Company. Here you will account for Canyon Canoe Company's transactions as it is actually done in practice. Begin by reviewing the transactions from Chapter 1 that are reprinted here:

Nov. 1   Amber Wilson invested $16,000 cash in the business by opening a bank account in the name of Canyon Canoe Company.

     2   The company leased a building and paid $1,200 for the first month's rent.

     3   The company purchased canoes for $4,800 on account.

     4   The company purchased office supplies on account, $750.

     7   The company earned $1,400 cash for the rental of canoes.

    13   The company paid $1,500 cash for salaries.

    15   Amber Wilson withdrew $50 cash from the business for personal use.

    16   The company received a bill for $150 for utilities, which will be paid later.

    20   The company received a bill for $175 for cellphone expenses. The bill will be paid later.

    22   The company rented canoes to Early Start Daycare on account, $3,000.

    26   Canyon Canoe Company paid $1,000 of the amount owed for the November 3 purchase that was made on account.

    28   The company received $750 from Early Start Daycare for canoe rental on November 22.

    30   Amber Wilson withdrew cash of $100 from the business for personal use.

In addition, Canyon Canoe Company completed the following transactions for December.

Dec. 1   Amber Wilson contributed land on the river (worth $85,000) and a small building to use as a rental office (worth $35,000) in exchange for owner's equity.

     1   The company prepaid $3,000 for three months' rent on the warehouse where the company stores the canoes. (Use the Prepaid Rent account.)

     2   The company purchased canoes, signing a note payable for $7,200.

     4   The company purchased office supplies on account for $500.

     9   The company received $4,500 cash for canoe rentals to customers.

    15   Canyon Canoe Company rented canoes to customers for $3,500, but will be paid next month.

    16   Canyon Canoe Company received a $750 rental deposit from a group that will use the canoes next month. (Use the Unearned Revenue account.)

    18   The company paid the utilities and telephone bills from last month.

    19   The company paid other accounts payable in the amount of $2,000.

    20   Canyon Canoe Company received bills for the telephone ($325) and utilities ($295), which will be paid later.

    31   The company paid salaries of $1,800.

    31   Amber Wilson withdrew $300 from the business for personal use.

Required

1. Journalize the transactions for both November and December, using the following accounts: Cash; Accounts Receivable; Office Supplies; Prepaid Rent; Land; Building; Canoes; Accounts Payable; Unearned Revenue; Note Payable; Amber Wilson, Capital; Amber Wilson, Withdrawals; Canoe Rental Revenue; Rent Expense; Salaries Expense; Utilities Expense; and Telephone Expense. Explanations are not required. (Hint: For November transactions, refer to your answer for E1-18 if you completed it.)

2. Open a T-account for each of these accounts in the order presented in requirement 1.

3. Post the journal entries to the T-accounts, and calculate account balances. Formal posting references are not required.

4. Prepare an unadjusted trial balance as of December 31, 2020.

5. Prepare the income statement of Canyon Canoe Company for the two months ended December 31, 2020. List expenses in this order: Rent Expense; Salaries Expense; Utilities Expense; and Telephone Expense.

6. Prepare the statement of owner's equity for the two months ended December 31, 2020.

7. Prepare the balance sheet as of December 31, 2020.

Requirement 1

	Journal				Page 1
DATE	ACCOUNT TITLES AND EXPLANATIONS	POST REF.	DEBIT	CREDIT	

Requirement 1 (Continued)

		Journal			Page 1
DATE		ACCOUNT TITLES AND EXPLANATIONS	POST REF.	DEBIT	CREDIT

Requirements 2 & 3

Cash

_____|_____

Accounts Receivable   Office Supplies

_____|_____   _____|_____

Prepaid Rent   Land

_____|_____   _____|_____

Building   Canoes

_____|_____   _____|_____

Accounts Payable   Unearned Revenue

_____|_____   _____|_____

Requirements 2 & 3 (Continued)

Note Payable	Amber Wilson, Capital

Amber Wilson, Withdrawals	Canoe Rental Revenue

Rent Expense	Salaries Expense

Utilities Expense	Telephone Expense

Requirement 4

ACCOUNT	DEBIT	CREDIT

Requirement 5

Income Statement		

Requirement 6

Statement of Owner's Equity		

Requirement 7

Balance Sheet			

		Extra Journal Paper			
DATE		ACCOUNTS TITLES AND EXPLANATIONS	POST REF.	DEBIT	CREDIT

P2–3A ② ③

Zeb Slipewicz opened a renovation business called WeReDoIt Construction on September 3, 2020. During the first month of operations, the business completed the following transactions:

Sep.	3	Slipewicz deposited a cheque for $72,000 into the business bank account to start the business.
	4	Purchased supplies, $600, and furniture, $4,400, on account.
	5	Paid September rent expense, $1,500 cash.
	6	Performed design services for a client and received $2,400 cash.
	7	Paid $44,000 cash to acquire land for a future office site.
	10	Designed a bathroom for a client, billed the client, and received her promise to pay the $5,800 within one week.
	14	Paid for the furniture purchased September 4 on account.
	15	Paid assistant's salary, $940 cash.
	17	Received cash on account, $3,400.
	22	Received $5,000 cash from a client for renovation of a cottage.
	25	Prepared a recreation room design for a client on account, $1,600.
	30	Paid assistant's salary, $940 cash.
	30	Slipewicz withdrew $5,600 cash for personal use.

Required Record each transaction in the journal with an explanation. Identify each transaction by date. Use the following accounts: Cash; Accounts Receivable; Supplies; Furniture; Land; Accounts Payable; Z. Slipewicz, Capital; Z. Slipewicz, Withdrawals; Service Revenue; Rent Expense; Salaries Expense.

Journal					Page 1
DATE		ACCOUNT TITLES AND EXPLANATIONS	POST REF.	DEBIT	CREDIT

		Journal			Page 2
DATE		ACCOUNT TITLES AND EXPLANATIONS	POST REF.	DEBIT	CREDIT

P2-4A ② ③ ④

The trial balance of Kiki's Jewellery Repair at February 29, 2020, is shown below:

	KIKI'S JEWELLERY REPAIR		
	Unadjusted Trial Balance		
	February 29, 2020		
Account Number	**Account Title**	**Debit**	**Credit**
1100	Cash	$ 4,000	
1200	Accounts receivable	16,000	
1300	Supplies	3,600	
1600	Equipment	37,200	
2000	Accounts payable		$ 8,000
3000	K. Kalani, Capital		50,000
3100	K. Kalani, Withdrawals	4,400	
5000	Service revenue		16,400
6100	Rent expense	2,000	
6200	Salary expense	7,200	
	Total	$74,400	$74,400

During March, Kiki's Jewellery Repair completed the following transactions:

Mar.	4	Collected $600 cash from a client on account.
	8	Provided an heirloom jewellery redesign service for a client on account, $580.
	13	Paid for items previously purchased on account, $320.
	18	Purchased supplies on account, $120.
	20	Kalani withdrew $200 cash for personal use.
	21	Received a verbal promise of a $200 commission.
	22	Received cash of $620 for work just completed.
	31	Paid employees' salaries, $1,300 cash.

Required

1. Record the March transactions in page 3 of the journal. Include an explanation for each entry.
2. Open three-column ledger accounts for the accounts listed in the trial balance, together with their balances at February 29. Enter Bal. (for previous balance) in the Item column, and place a check mark (✓) in the journal reference column for the February 29 balance in each account.
3. Post the transactions to the ledger, using dates, account numbers, journal references, and posting references.

Requirement 1

	Journal			Page 3
DATE	ACCOUNT TITLES AND EXPLANATIONS	POST REF.	DEBIT	CREDIT

Requirements 2 & 3

ACCOUNT:	CASH				ACCOUNT NO. 1100
DATE	ITEM	JRNL. REF.	DEBIT	CREDIT	BALANCE

ACCOUNT	ACCOUNTS RECEIVABLE				ACCOUNT NO. 1200
DATE	ITEM	JRNL. REF.	DEBIT	CREDIT	BALANCE

ACCOUNT	SUPPLIES				ACCOUNT NO. 1300
DATE	ITEM	JRNL. REF.	DEBIT	CREDIT	BALANCE

ACCOUNT	EQUIPMENT				ACCOUNT NO. 1600
DATE	ITEM	JRNL. REF.	DEBIT	CREDIT	BALANCE

Requirements 2 & 3 (Continued)

ACCOUNT	ACCOUNTS PAYABLE				ACCOUNT NO. 2000
DATE	ITEM	JRNL. REF.	DEBIT	CREDIT	BALANCE

ACCOUNT	K. KALANI, CAPITAL				ACCOUNT NO. 3000
DATE	ITEM	JRNL. REF.	DEBIT	CREDIT	BALANCE

ACCOUNT	K. KALANI, WITHDRAWALS				ACCOUNT NO. 3100
DATE	ITEM	JRNL. REF.	DEBIT	CREDIT	BALANCE

ACCOUNT	SERVICE REVENUE				ACCOUNT NO. 5000
DATE	ITEM	JRNL. REF.	DEBIT	CREDIT	BALANCE

ACCOUNT	RENT EXPENSE				ACCOUNT NO. 6100
DATE	ITEM	JRNL. REF.	DEBIT	CREDIT	BALANCE

Requirements 2 & 3 (Continued)

ACCOUNT SALARIES EXPENSE					ACCOUNT NO. 6200
DATE	ITEM	JRNL. REF.	DEBIT	CREDIT	BALANCE

P2–5A ② ③ ④ ⑤

Sophie Vaillancourt started an investment management business, Vaillancourt Management, on June 1, 2020. During the first month of operations, the business completed the following selected transactions:

Jun. 1   Vaillancourt began the business with an investment of $20,000 cash, land valued at $60,000, and a building valued at $120,000. The business gave her owner's equity in the business for the value of the cash, land, and building. (Hint: This is a compound journal entry.)

3   Purchased office supplies on account, $2,600.

4   Paid $15,000 cash for office furniture.

12   Paid employee salary, $2,200 cash.

15   Performed consulting service on account for clients, $12,100.

22   Paid in cash $800 of the account payable created by purchasing office supplies on June 3.

24   Received a $2,000 bill for advertising expense that will be paid in the near future.

25   Performed consulting services for customers and received cash, $5,600.

26   Received cash on account, $2,400.

29   Paid the following expenses with two separate cheques:

(1) Rent of photocopier, $1,700.

(2) Utilities, $400.

30   Vaillancourt withdrew $6,500 cash for personal use.

Required

1. Record each transaction in the journal.
2. Open the following three-column ledger accounts: Cash, #1100; Accounts Receivable, #1300; Office Supplies, #1400; Office Furniture, #1500; Building, #1700; Land, #1800; Accounts Payable, #2100; Sophie Vaillancourt, Capital, #3100; Sophie Vaillancourt, Withdrawals, #3200; Service Revenue, #4100; Advertising Expense, #5100; Equipment Rental Expense, #5300; Salaries Expense, #5500; Utilities Expense, #5700.
3. Post to the accounts and keep a running balance for each account.
4. Prepare the unadjusted trial balance of Vaillancourt Management at June 30, 2020.

Requirement 1

Journal					
DATE		ACCOUNT TITLES AND EXPLANATIONS	POST REF.	DEBIT	CREDIT

Requirement 1 (Continued)

\multicolumn{6}{c|}{**Journal**}

DATE		ACCOUNT TITLES AND EXPLANATIONS	POST REF.	DEBIT	CREDIT

Requirements 2 & 3

ACCOUNT	CASH					ACCOUNT NO. 1100
DATE		ITEM	JRNL. REF.	DEBIT	CREDIT	BALANCE

ACCOUNT	ACCOUNTS RECEIVABLE					ACCOUNT NO. 1300
DATE		ITEM	JRNL. REF.	DEBIT	CREDIT	BALANCE

ACCOUNT	OFFICE SUPPLIES					ACCOUNT NO. 1400
DATE		ITEM	JRNL. REF.	DEBIT	CREDIT	BALANCE

ACCOUNT	OFFICE FURNITURE					ACCOUNT NO. 1500
DATE		ITEM	JRNL. REF.	DEBIT	CREDIT	BALANCE

Requirements 2 & 3 (Continued)

ACCOUNT	BUILDING				ACCOUNT NO. 1700	
DATE		ITEM	JRNL. REF.	DEBIT	CREDIT	BALANCE

ACCOUNT	LAND				ACCOUNT NO. 1800	
DATE		ITEM	JRNL. REF.	DEBIT	CREDIT	BALANCE

ACCOUNT	ACCOUNTS PAYABLE				ACCOUNT NO. 2100	
DATE		ITEM	JRNL. REF.	DEBIT	CREDIT	BALANCE

ACCOUNT	SOPHIE VAILLANCOURT, CAPITAL				ACCOUNT NO. 3100	
DATE		ITEM	JRNL. REF.	DEBIT	CREDIT	BALANCE

ACCOUNT	SOPHIE VAILLANCOURT, WITHDRAWALS				ACCOUNT NO. 3200	
DATE		ITEM	JRNL. REF.	DEBIT	CREDIT	BALANCE

Requirements 2 & 3 (Continued)

ACCOUNT	SERVICE REVENUE				ACCOUNT NO. 4100
DATE	ITEM	JRNL. REF.	DEBIT	CREDIT	BALANCE

ACCOUNT	ADVERTISING EXPENSE				ACCOUNT NO. 5100
DATE	ITEM	JRNL. REF.	DEBIT	CREDIT	BALANCE

ACCOUNT	EQUIPMENT RENTAL EXPENSE				ACCOUNT NO. 5300
DATE	ITEM	JRNL. REF.	DEBIT	CREDIT	BALANCE

ACCOUNT	SALARIES EXPENSE				ACCOUNT NO. 5500
DATE	ITEM	JRNL. REF.	DEBIT	CREDIT	BALANCE

ACCOUNT	UTILITIES EXPENSE				ACCOUNT NO. 5700
DATE	ITEM	JRNL. REF.	DEBIT	CREDIT	BALANCE

Requirement 4

	Unadjusted Trial Balance		
ACCT. NO.	ACCOUNT	DEBIT	CREDIT

Extra Journal Paper

DATE		ACCOUNTS TITLES AND EXPLANATIONS	POST REF.	DEBIT	CREDIT

P2–6A ② ⑤

The following trial balance does not balance:

A-PLUS TRAVEL PLANNERS		
Unadjusted Trial Balance		
June 30, 2020		
Cash	$ 1,600	
Accounts receivable	10,000	
Supplies	900	
Office furniture	3,600	
Land	46,600	
Accounts payable		$ 3,800
Note payable		23,000
R. Minter, capital		31,600
R. Minter, withdrawals	2,000	
Consulting service revenue		7,300
Advertising expense	400	
Rent expense	1,000	
Salaries expense	2,100	
Utilities expense	410	
Total	$68,610	$65,700

The following errors were detected:

a. The cash balance is understated by $1,300.

b. The cost of the land was $44,600, not $46,600.

c. A $400 purchase of supplies on account was neither journalized nor posted.

d. A $3,000 credit to Consulting Service Revenue was not posted.

e. Rent Expense of $200 was posted as a credit rather than a debit.

f. The balance of Advertising Expense is $600, but it was listed as $400 on the trial balance.

g. A $300 debit to Accounts Receivable was posted as $30. The credit to Consulting Service Revenue was correct.

h. The balance of Utilities Expense is overstated by $80.

i. A $900 debit to the R. Minter, Withdrawals account was posted as a debit to R. Minter, Capital.

Required   Prepare the corrected unadjusted trial balance at June 30, 2020. Journal entries are not required.

Unadjusted Trial Balance		
ACCOUNT	DEBIT	CREDIT

Calculations:

P2–7A ② ③ ④ ⑤

Canada-Wide Movers had the following account balances, in random order, on December 15, 2020 (all accounts have their "normal" balances):

Moving fees income....................	$259,800	Cash...	$ 17,200
Accounts receivable....................	7,400	Storage fees income.................	57,900
Rent expense...............................	47,100	Note receivable........................	45,000
H. Martinez, capital....................	53,000	Utilities expense......................	2,400
Office supplies expense.............	2,100	Office supplies..........................	9,600
Mortgage payable.......................	39,000	Accounts payable.....................	33,000
Salaries expense.........................	161,100	Office equipment......................	12,300
Insurance expense......................	6,300	Moving equipment...................	132,200

The following events took place during the final weeks of the year:

Dec. 17   Moved a customer's goods to Canada-Wide's rented warehouse for storage. The moving fees were $4,000. Storage fees are $600 per month. The customer was billed for 1 month's storage and the moving fees.

18   Collected a $15,000 note owed to Canada-Wide Movers and collected interest income of $1,800 cash.

19   Used a company cheque to pay for Martinez's personal hydro bill in the amount of $400.

21   Purchased storage racks for $12,000. Paid $3,600 cash, provided moving services for $1,500, and promised to pay the balance in 60 days.

23   Collected $3,000 cash; $2,600 of this was for moving goods on December 15 (recorded as an account receivable at that time), and the balance was for storage fees for the period of December 16 to 23.

24   Canada-Wide Movers paid cash of $18,000 owing on the mortgage.

27   Martinez withdrew $5,000 cash for personal use.

29   Provided moving services to a lawyer for $2,400. The lawyer paid Canada-Wide Movers $1,500 and provided legal work for the balance.

31   Martinez, the owner of Canada-Wide Movers, sold 2,000 shares he held in Brandon Haulage Inc. for $12,000.

Required

1. Where appropriate, record each transaction from December 17 to 31 in the journal. Include an explanation for each journal entry.

2. Enter December 15 balances in the T-accounts.

3. Post entries in T-accounts and calculate the balance of each one.

4. Prepare the unadjusted trial balance of Canada-Wide Movers at December 31, 2020.

Requirement 1

Journal

DATE		ACCOUNT TITLES AND EXPLANATIONS	POST REF.	DEBIT	CREDIT

Requirement 1 (Continued)

		Journal		
DATE		ACCOUNT TITLES AND EXPLANATIONS	POST REF.	DEBIT	CREDIT

Requirement 2

Cash

Accounts Receivable

Notes Receivable

Office Supplies

Office Equipment

Moving Equipment

Storage Equipment

Accounts Payable

Mortgage Payable

H. Martinez, Capital

Requirement 2 (Continued)

H. Martinez, Withdrawals	Moving Fees Income

Storage Fees Income	Interest Income

Insurance Expense	Legal Expense

Office Supplies Expense	Rent Expense

Salaries Expense	Utilities Expense

Requirement 3

Unadjusted Trial Balance		
ACCOUNT	DEBIT	CREDIT

Extra Journal Paper

DATE		ACCOUNTS TITLES AND EXPLANATIONS	POST REF.	DEBIT	CREDIT

3 MEASURING BUSINESS INCOME: THE ADJUSTING PROCESS

LEARNING OBJECTIVES

1 Apply the recognition criteria for revenues and expenses.
2 Distinguish accrual-basis accounting from cash-basis accounting.
3 Prepare adjusting entries.
4 Prepare an adjusted trial balance.
5 Prepare the financial statements from the adjusted trial balance.
6 Describe the adjusting-process implications of International Financial Reporting Standards (IFRS).

*A1 Account for a prepaid expense recorded initially as an expense.
*A2 Account for an unearned revenue recorded initially as a revenue.

SOME USEFUL TEXT INFORMATION (add your own notes too)

Two rules to remember about adjusting entries:

1. Adjusting entries never involve the Cash account.

2. Adjusting entries either
   a. increase a revenue account (credit revenue) or
   b. increase an expense account (debit expense)

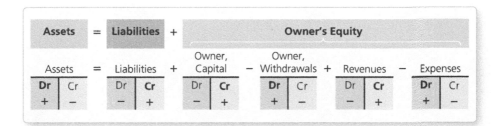

Assets		=	Liabilities	+			Owner's Equity					
Assets		=	Liabilities	+	Owner, Capital	−	Owner, Withdrawals	+	Revenues	−	Expenses	
Dr	Cr	=	Dr	**Cr**	Dr	**Cr**	**Dr**	Cr	Dr	**Cr**	**Dr**	Cr
+	−		−	+	−	+	+	−	−	+	+	−

EXHIBIT 3–7 | Timing of Prepaid and Accrual Adjustments

PREPAIDS—Cash receipt or cash payment occurs first

	ORIGINAL ENTRY			ADJUSTING ENTRY		
Prepaid expenses	Prepaid Insurance	xxx		Insurance Expense	xxx	
	Cash		xxx	Prepaid Insurance		xxx
	Pay for insurance in advance and record an asset first.			Adjust for insurance used later and decrease the asset.		
Amortization	Furniture	xxx		Amortization Expense—Furniture	xxx	
	Cash		xxx	Accum. Amort.—Furniture		xxx
	Pay for furniture in advance and record an asset first.			Adjust for amortization (use) of asset later.		
Unearned revenues	Cash	xxx		Unearned Revenue	xxx	
	Unearned Revenue		xxx	Revenue (e.g., Consulting)		xxx
	Receive cash in advance and record a liability first.			Adjust for revenue earned later and decrease the liability.		

ACCRUALS—Cash receipt or cash payment occurs later.

	ADJUSTING ENTRY			LATER ENTRY		
Accrued expenses	Salaries Expense	xxx		Salaries Payable	xxx	
	Salaries Payable		xxx	Cash		xxx
	Accrue for expense first and increase liability.			Pay the liability later.		
Accrued revenues	Accounts Receivable	xxx		Cash	xxx	
	Revenue (e.g., Consulting)		xxx	Accounts Receivable		xxx
	Accrue the revenue earned first and increase the receivable.			Collect cash from the customer later.		

S3–4 ②

Suppose you house-sit for people while they are away on vacation. Most of your customers pay you immediately after you finish a job. A few ask you to send them a bill. It is now June 30, and you have collected $600 from cash-paying customers. Your remaining customers owe you $1,400. How much service revenue would you have under the (a) cash basis and (b) accrual basis of accounting? Which method of accounting provides more information about your house-sitting business? Explain your answer.

a.

b.

S3–8 ③

On April 1, 2020, you prepaid three months of rent for a total of $18,000. Give your adjusting entry to record rent expense at April 30, 2020. Include the date of the entry and an explanation. Then, using T-accounts, post to the two accounts involved and show their balances at April 30, 2020.

Journal					
DATE		ACCOUNT TITLES AND EXPLANATIONS	POST REF.	DEBIT	CREDIT
Apr	1	Rent Prepaid		18000	
		Cash			18000
		Rent prepaid (3 months)			

Rent Expense

APR 30	6000	
1 may	6000	

Rent Prepaid a/c

APR 1 Cash 18000	APR 30 Rent Exp 6000
1 may 12000	

S3-9 ③

At the beginning of the month, Supplies were $500. During the month, the company purchased $600 of supplies. At month's end, November 30, $400 of supplies were still on hand.

a. What was the cost of supplies used during the month? Where is this item reported?

b. Where is the ending balance of supplies reported?

c. Make the adjusting entry to update the Supplies account at the end of the month.

	Journal				
DATE	ACCOUNT TITLES AND EXPLANATIONS	POST REF.	DEBIT	CREDIT
	Supplies		600	
	Cash			600
30 Nov	Supplies exp		700	
	Supplies			700 .

S3-10 ③

On May 1 your company paid cash of $27,000 for computers that are expected to remain useful for three years. At the end of three years, the value of the computers is expected to be zero. (Hint: Use the formula found on page 122 of your textbook.)

Make journal entries to record (a) the purchase of the computers on May 1 and (b) amortization on May 31. Include dates and explanations, and use the following accounts: Computer Equipment, Accumulated Amortization—Computer Equipment, and Amortization Expense—Computer Equipment.

	Journal				
DATE	ACCOUNT TITLES AND EXPLANATIONS	POST REF.	DEBIT	CREDIT
May 1	Computer Equipment		27000	
	Cash			27000 .
May 31	Amortization Expense - Comp.		750	
	Accumulated Amortization			750

S3–11 ③

Refer to the data in S3–10.

1. Using T-accounts, post to the accounts listed in S3–10 and show their balances at May 31.
2. What is the computer equipment's book value at May 31?
3. What amount is reported on the income statement on May 31?

①

Cash.
may 27000	

Computer Equipment
may 27000	

Amortisation Expense - Computer
31 may 750	

Accumulated Amortisation
	31 may 750

② Computer book value = 27000 - 750 = $ 26 250.00

③ Income statement reports an expense of $ 750 amortisation expense.

S3-12 ③

Suppose Resort Travel borrowed $60,000 on March 1 by signing a note payable to Royal Bank. Resort Travel's interest expense on the note payable for the remainder of its fiscal year (March through May) is $600.

1. Record Resort Travel's adjusting entry to accrue interest expense at May 31.
2. Post the adjusting entry to the T-accounts of the two accounts affected by the adjustment.

	Journal				
DATE	ACCOUNT TITLES AND EXPLANATIONS	POST REF.	DEBIT	CREDIT	
Mar 1	Cash		60 000		
	Note Payable			60 000	
May 31	Interest Expenses		600		
	Interest Payable			600	

S3-13 ③

Employees of Ralph's Llama Farm work Monday through Friday and are paid every Friday for work done that week. The daily payroll is $13,900 and the last payday was Friday, December 28. What is the required adjusting journal entry, if any, on Monday, December 31?

	Journal				
DATE	ACCOUNT TITLES AND EXPLANATIONS	POST REF.	DEBIT	CREDIT	
28 Dec	Salary Expense		13 900		
	Salaries Payable			13 900	
extra from sir					
Jan 4	Salary Payable		13 900		
	Salary Expenses		55 600		
	Cash			69 500	

S3-14 ③

Shell Collector magazine collects cash from subscribers in advance and then mails the magazines to subscribers over a one-year period. Give the adjusting entry that the company makes to record the earning of $10,000 of subscription revenue that was collected in advance on March 1, 2020.

	Journal				
DATE	ACCOUNT TITLES AND EXPLANATIONS	POST REF.	DEBIT	CREDIT	
Mar	Cash		10 000		
	Unearned revenue			10 000	
1 Sep	Unearned revenue		5000		
	Service Revenue			5000	

S3–15 ③

TentRentals Company sets up a large event tent for the local food festival. The tent will be rented to the Business Improvement Association for two weeks for a total cost of $3,500. The event takes place over the Canada Day weekend. So one week of the rental takes place in June, and the other week is in July. TentRentals will bill the Business Improvement Association on July 6 for the two-week rental. Record the June 30 adjusting entry to update TentRental's financial records for the one week they have earned rental revenue.

Journal

DATE		ACCOUNT TITLES AND EXPLANATIONS	POST REF.	DEBIT	CREDIT

S3–16 ④

Blazing Software Consulting had the following accounts and account balances after adjusting entries. Assume all accounts have normal balances. Prepare the adjusted trial balance for Blazing Software Consulting's year-end of September 30, 2020.

① Cash	$18,150	⑤ Computer Equipment	$15,000
⑷ Land	20,000	② Accounts Receivable	2,250
⑥ Utilities Payable	350	③ Office Supplies	200
⑺ Accounts Payable	3,100	⑧ S. Scott, Capital	18,400
Accumulated Amortization—Equipment	2,400	⑪ Utilities Expense	750
⑨ Service Revenue	60,000	Unearned Revenue	600
⑩ Supplies Expense	800	⑫ Amortization Expense—Equipment	1,200
S. Scott, Withdrawals	22,000	⑬ Salaries Expense	4,500

(handwritten trial balance)

Blazing Software Consulting
Adjusted Trial Balance
for the year end 30 September 2020

ACCOUNT	DEBIT	CREDIT
Cash	18 150	
A/R	2250	
Office Supplies	200	
Land	20 000	
Computer Equip (20000 – 2400)	12 600	
Utilities Payable		350
A/P		3 100
Scott Capital (18400 – 22000)	3 600	
Service rev (60000 + 600)		60 600
Supplies expense	800	
Utilities exps.	750	
Amort expen – equip.	1200	
Salaries exps	4500	
	64 050	64 050

$ 64 050

S3-19 ⑥

Do International Financial Reporting Standards (IFRS) for publicly accountable enterprises in Canada have an impact on the adjusting process for these companies?

_____

_____

_____

_____

_____

_____

_____

_____

_____

_____

_____

_____

*S3-20 Ⓐ①

On July 31, 2020, Magnus's Muffins paid $18,000 for business insurance for the next year. Record the entries for the purchase of the insurance by recording it as an expense and then making a year-end entry on December 31, 2020, to adjust the accounts.

	Journal				
DATE	ACCOUNT TITLES AND EXPLANATIONS	POST REF.	DEBIT	CREDIT	

*S3–21 (A2)

On November 1, 2020, Freya Albatter's orthodontic office received a $2,500 prepayment from a client for dental work to be performed on November 22. The appointment got postponed until January 15, 2021. Prepare the journal entries for November 1, the December 31 year-end, and the January 15 appointment dates. Assume that the prepayment was recorded as a revenue because, at that time, it was assumed the work would be performed within the month.

Journal					
DATE		ACCOUNT TITLES AND EXPLANATIONS	POST REF.	DEBIT	CREDIT

E3–1 (1)

Identify the accounting assumption, criteria, or objective that gives the most direction on how to account for each of the following situations:

a. The owner of a business desires monthly financial statements to measure the financial progress of the business on an ongoing basis.

b. Expenses of $3,000 must be accrued at the end of the period to measure income properly.

c. A customer states her intention to switch travel agencies. Should the new travel agency record revenue based on this intention? Give the reason for your answer.

d. Expenses of the period total $6,000. This amount should be subtracted from revenue to compute the period's net income.

E3–5 ③

Compute the missing amounts and insert them in the shaded areas for each of the following Prepaid Rent situations. For situation A, make the needed journal entry. Consider each situation separately.

Situation

	A	B	C	D	E
Beginning Prepaid Rent	$ 4,200	$ 5,000	$16,800	$5,900	
Payments for Prepaid Rent during the year	19,800		15,000		2,500
Total amount to account for			31,800	15,600	
Ending Prepaid Rent	19,000	6,000		6,000	1,400
Rent Expense		$12,000	$25,000	$9,600	$2,600

Calculations:

Journal entry for A

Journal					
DATE	ACCOUNTS TITLES AND EXPLANATIONS	POST REF.	DEBIT	CREDIT	

E3–8 ③

Journalize the adjusting entry needed at December 31 for each of the following independent situations:

a. On June 1, when we collected $48,000 rent in advance, we debited Cash and credited Unearned Rent Revenue. The tenant was paying for one year's rent in advance. At December 31, we must account for the amount of rent we have earned.

b. Interest revenue of $2,400 has been earned but not yet received on a $60,000 note receivable held by the business.

c. Salaries expense is $7,500 per day—Monday through Friday—and the business pays employees each Friday. This year December 31 falls on a Wednesday.

d. Equipment was purchased last year at a cost of $200,000. The equipment's useful life is five years. It will have no value after five years. Record the year's amortization.

e. On September 1, when we paid $6,000 for a one-year insurance policy, we debited Prepaid Insurance and credited Cash.

f. The business owes interest expense of $7,200 that it will pay early in the next period.

g. The unadjusted balance of the Supplies account is $13,500. The total cost of supplies remaining on hand on December 31 is $4,500.

	DATE	ACCOUNT TITLES AND EXPLANATIONS	POST REF.	DEBIT	CREDIT
		Journal			
(a)	31 Dec	Unearned Revenue		28 000	
		Revenue - Rent			28 000
(b)	31 Dec	Interest receivable		2400	
		Unearned revenue			2400
(c)	31 Dec	Salaries expenses		22 500	
		Salaries payable			22 500
(d)	31 Dec	Amortization Expense-Equip		40 000	
		Accumulated Amortization			40 000
(e)	31 Dec	Insurance expenses		2 000	
		Prepaid insurance			2 000
(f)	31 Dec	Interest expense		7 200	
		Interest payable			7 200
(g)	31 Dec	Supplies expense		9 000	
		Supplies			9 000

*g — Dec 31   Cash   6000
            A/c receivable   6000

E3-9 ③

Journalize the following December 31 transactions for Jieun Printing Services. No explanations are required.

a. Equipment cost is $24,000 and is expected to be useful for 10 years, at which time it will have no residual value. Calculate and record amortization for the current year.

b. Each Monday, Jieun pays employees for the previous week's work. The amount of weekly payroll is $5,600 for a seven-day workweek (Monday to Sunday). This year December 31 falls on a Thursday.

c. The beginning balance of Supplies was $2,500. During the year, Jieun purchased supplies for $3,000, and at December 31 the supplies on hand totalled $1,700.

d. Jieun prepaid one year of insurance coverage on August 1 of the current year, $5,280. Record insurance expense for the year ended December 31.

e. Jieun earned $3,200 of unearned revenue.

f. Jieun incurred $150 of interest expense on a note payable that will not be paid until February 28.

g. Jieun billed customers $6,000 for printing services performed.

	Journal				
DATE		ACCOUNT TITLES AND EXPLANATIONS	POST REF.	DEBIT	CREDIT
a Jan	1	Equipment		24 000	
		Cash			24 000
Dec	31	Amortization exp - equipment		2400	
		Acc. amortization			2400
b Dec	31	Salaries expense		3200	
		Salaries payable			3200
c Jan	1	Supplies		3000	
		Cash			3000
Dec	31	Supplies expense		3800	
		Supplies			3800
d Aug	1	Insurance prepaid		5280	
		Cash			5280
Dec	31	Insurance expense		2200	
		Insurance p.p.			2200
e Jan	1	Cash		3200	
		Unearned revenue			3200
Dec 31		Unearned revenue		3200	
Calculations:		Service revenue			3200
f Jan 1		Interest expense		150	
		Interest payable			150
g Jan 1		Account receivable		6000	
⊛		Service revenue			6000

HW

Measuring Business Income: The Adjusting Proce—

E3-10 ③

For each of these six independent situations, journalize the adjusting entry and the related transaction (either before or after it):

a. Dec. 1 – business receives $2,000 for a 10-month service contract.
   Dec. 31 – year-end adjusting entry needed to update the balance in the account.

b. Mar. 31 – work performed but not yet billed to customers for the month, $900.
   Apr. 21 – received payment for the work that was completed.

c. Jun. 15 – purchased $3,500 of office supplies on account.
   Dec. 31 – a count of supplies shows that only $1,700 worth is left at year-end, so the balance in the account needs to be updated.

d. Feb. 2 – business paid a $450 deposit for the last month's rental of a copier on a 10-month contract.
   Nov. 30 – the rental period for the copier ended, so the balance in the prepaid account must be updated.

e. Jun. 1 – purchased truck for $39,900 (cash) with an expected useful life of seven years.

f. Dec. 31 – year-end adjusting entry needed to record amortization.

	DATE		ACCOUNT TITLES AND EXPLANATIONS	POST REF.	DEBIT	CREDIT
	\multicolumn{2}{c}{**Journal**}				

	DATE		ACCOUNT TITLES AND EXPLANATIONS	POST REF.	DEBIT	CREDIT
(a)	Dec	1	Cash		2000	
			Unearned revenue			2000
	Dec	31	Unearned revenue		200	
			Service revenue			200
(b)	Mar	31	A/c payable		900	
			Service revenue			900
	Apr	21	Cash		900	
			A/c receivable			900
(c)	June	15	Office supplies		3500	
			A/c payable			3500
	Dec	31	Off. supplies expense		1800	
			Supplies			1800
(d)	Feb	2	Prepaid Rent – copier		450	
			Cash			450
	Nov	30	Rent expense		450	
			PP. Rent			450
(e)	June	1	Truck		39900	
			Cash			39900
(f)	Dec	31	Amortization Exp.		3325	
			Acc. Amortization			3325

Journal

DATE		ACCOUNT TITLES AND EXPLANATIONS	POST REF.	DEBIT	CREDIT

Calculations:

H/W

Measuring Business Income: The

96

E3–14 ④

Prepare an adjusted trial balance for Toronto Mobile Pet Grooming as at June 30, 2020. Assume that all accounts have the~~ ~~
balances. List expenses in alphabetical order.

Accounts payable...... L	$ 4,000	Assets
Accumulated amortization—truck... L X Assets	7,000	Liabilities
Amortization expense—truck... E	1,000	
Cash... A	2,400	Owner's Capital
Truck... A	40,000	Revenue
Insurance expense... E	200	Expense
Les Birman, capital... OE	17,000	
Les Birman, withdrawals... OE	8,000	
Prepaid insurance... A	1,800	
Salaries expense... E	16,000	
Salaries payable... L	2,000	
Service revenue... R	44,000	
Grooming supplies... A	4,000	
Supplies expense... E	2,000	
Unearned service revenue... L	1,400	

A
L
O
R
E

Toronto Mobile Pet Grooming
Adjusted Trial Balance
as at 30 June 2020

ACCOUNT	DEBIT	CREDIT
1. Cash	2 400	
2. Grooming supplies	4 000	
3. Prepaid insurance	1 800	
4. Truck	40 000	
5. Accounts payable		4 000
6. Salaries payable		2 000
7. Unearned service revenue		1 400
8. Accumulated amortization - Truck		7 000
9. Les Birman, capital		17 000
10. Les Birman, withdrawal	8 000	
11. Service revenue		44 000
12. Supplies expense	2 000	
13. Insurance expense	200	
14. Salaries expense	16 000	
15. Amortization expenses	1 000	
Total	75 400	75 400

75 400

3–15 ⑤

Refer to the data in E3–14. Prepare Toronto Mobile Pet Grooming's income statement and statement of owner's equity for the year ended June 30, 2020. Then prepare the balance sheet on that date.

Income Statement		

$24 800

Statement of Owner's Equity		

$ 33 800

Balance Sheet			

$41 200.

Extra Journal Page

DATE		ACCOUNTS TITLES AND EXPLANATIONS	POST REF.	DEBIT	CREDIT

E3-20 ③ ④ Serial Exercise

The Serial Exercise involves a company that will be revisited throughout relevant chapters in Volume 1 and Volume 2. You can complete the Serial Exercises using MyLab Accounting.

This exercise continues recordkeeping for the Canyon Canoe Company from previous chapters. You will need to use the unadjusted trial balance and posted T-accounts that you prepared in Chapter 2. If you did not complete the previous question, you can still work through this question using the following unadjusted trial balance:

CANYON CANOE COMPANY		
Unadjusted Trial Balance		
December 31, 2020		
Account Title	**Debits**	**Credits**
Cash	$ 12,125	
Accounts receivable	5,750	
Office supplies	1,250	
Prepaid rent	3,000	
Land	85,000	
Building	35,000	
Canoes	12,000	
Accounts payable		$ 3,670
Unearned revenue		750
Note payable		7,200
Amber Wilson, capital		136,000
Amber Wilson, withdrawals	450	
Canoe rental revenue		12,400
Rent expense	1,200	
Salaries expense	3,300	
Utilities expense	445	
Telephone expense	500	
Total	$160,020	$160,020

At December 31, the business gathers the following information for the adjusting entries:

a. At December 31, the office supplies on hand totaled $165.

b. Prepaid rent of one month has been used. (Hint: Total is for three months.)

c. Determine the amortization on the building using straight-line amortization. Assume the useful life of the building is five years and the residual value is $5,000. (Hint: The building was purchased on December 1.)

d. $400 of unearned revenue has now been earned.

e. The employee who has been working the rental booth has earned $1,250 in salaries that will be paid January 15, 2021.

f. Canyon Canoe Company has earned $1,850 of canoe rental revenue that has not been recorded or received.

g. Determine the amortization on the canoes purchased on November 3 using the straight-line method. Assume the useful life of the canoes is four years and the residual value is $0.

h. Determine the amortization on the canoes purchased on December 2 using the straight-line amortization method. Assume the useful life of the canoes is four years and the residual value is $0.

i. Interest expense of $50 has accrued on the note payable.

Required

1. Journalize and post the adjusting entries. In the T-accounts, denote each adjusting amount as *Adj.* and an account balance as *Bal. You may require new T-accounts*. If you did not complete E2-22 then open and post to only the t-accounts which required adjusting entries.
2. Prepare an adjusted trial balance as of December 31, 2020. Add new accounts in the order they appear in the journal entries.

Requirement 1

	Journal				
DATE		ACCOUNTS TITLES AND EXPLANATIONS	POST REF.	DEBIT	CREDIT

Requirement 1 (Continued)

Cash

Nov. 1	16,000	Nov. 2	1,200
Nov. 7	1,400	Nov. 13	1,500
Nov. 28	750	Nov. 15	50
Dec. 9	4,500	Nov. 26	1,000
Dec. 16	750	Nov. 30	100
		Dec. 1	3,000
		Dec. 18	325
		Dec. 19	2,000
		Dec. 31	1,800
		Dec. 31	300

Accounts Receivable

Nov. 22	3,000	Nov. 28	750
Dec. 15	3,500		

Office Supplies

Nov. 4	750		
Dec. 4	500		

Prepaid Rent

Dec. 1	3,000		

Land

Dec. 1	85,000		

Requirement 1 (Continued)

Building

Dec. 1	35,000		

Accumulated Amortization—Building

Canoes

Nov. 3	4,800		
Dec. 2	7,200		

Accumulated Amortization—Canoes

Accounts Payable

Dec. 18	150	Nov. 4	750
Dec. 18	175	Nov. 16	150
Dec. 19	2,000	Nov. 20	175
		Dec. 4	500
		Dec. 20	325
		Dec. 20	295

Requirement 1 (Continued)

Unearned Revenue

	Dec. 16	750

Salaries Payable

Interest Payable

Note Payable

	Dec. 2	7,200

Amber Wilson, Capital

	Nov. 1	16,000
	Dec. 1	120,000

Amber Wilson, Withdrawals

Nov. 15	50	
Nov. 30	100	
Dec. 31	300	

Requirement 1 (Continued)

Canoe Rental Revenue			
	Nov. 7	1,400
	Nov. 22	3,000
	Dec. 9	4,500
	Dec. 15	3,500

Rent Expense			
Nov. 2	1,200		

Salaries Expense			
Nov. 13	1,500		
Dec. 31	1,800		

Utilities Expense			
Nov. 16	150		
Dec. 20	295		

Telephone Expense			
Nov. 20	175		
Dec. 20	325		

Requirement 1 (Continued)

Supplies Expense
_____|_____

Amortization Expense—Building
_____|_____

Amortization Expense—Canoes
_____|_____

Interest Expense
_____|_____

Requirement 2

ACCOUNT	DEBIT	CREDIT

P3-3A ③

Journalize the adjusting entry needed on December 31, the company's year-end, for each of the following independent cases affecting Envision Communications:

a. The beginning balance of Supplies was $4,800. During the year the company purchased supplies costing $7,600, and at December 31 the inventory of supplies remaining on hand is $3,200.

b. Each Friday the company pays its employees for the current week's work. The amount of the payroll is $15,000 for a five-day workweek. The current accounting period ends on Wednesday.

c. Envision has received notes receivable from some clients for professional services. During the current year, Envision has earned interest revenue of $800, which will be received next year.

d. The company is developing a wireless communication system for a large company, and the client paid Envision $120,000 at the start of the project. Envision recorded this amount as Unearned Consulting Revenue. The development will take several months to complete. Envision executives estimate that the company has earned three-fourths of the total fee during the current year.

e. Amortization for the current year includes the following: Office Furniture, $8,600, and Design Equipment, $16,000. Make a compound entry. (Hint: This means showing everything in one journal entry, not two.)

f. Details of Prepaid Insurance are shown in the account:

Prepaid Insurance		
Jan. 2 Bal.	6,000	

Envision Communications prepays a full year's insurance on January 2. Record insurance expense for the year ended December 31 as one annual adjustment for what was used for the year.

Calculations:

a. – f.

		ACCOUNTS TITLES AND EXPLANATIONS	POST REF.	DEBIT	CREDIT
DATE					

Journal

P3–4A ③

FancyJohns, the luxury portable toilet rental company, has collected the following data for the December 31 adjusting entries:

a. Each Friday, FancyJohns pays employees for the current week's work. The amount of the weekly payroll is $7,000 for a five-day workweek. This year December 31 falls on a Wednesday. FancyJohns will pay its employees on January 2.

b. On January 1 of the current year, FancyJohns purchased an insurance policy that covers two years, $19,000.

c. The beginning balance of Cleaning Supplies was $4,000. During the year, FancyJohns purchased cleaning supplies for $5,200, and at December 31 the cleaning supplies on hand total $2,400.

d. During December, FancyJohns arranged for rentals at a Christmas and a New Year's Eve party at a resort. The client prepaid $7,000. FancyJohns recorded this amount as Unearned Revenue. FancyJohns estimates that the company has earned 45 percent of the total revenue in the current year and will earn the balance on January 3.

e. At December 31, FancyJohns had earned $3,500 of a two-month rental at the Outdoor Ice Place. The Outdoor Ice Palce has stated that they will pay FancyJohns the entire balance due for the two months on February 1.

f. Amortization for the current year includes Equipment, $3,700, and Trucks, $1,300. Make one compound entry to record the amortization, but use separate amortization accounts for each asset.

g. FancyJohns has incurred $300 of interest expense on a $450 interest payment due on January 15.

Required

1. Journalize the adjusting entry needed on December 31 for each of the previous items affecting FancyJohns. Assume FancyJohns records adjusting entries only at the end of the year.

2. Journalize the subsequent journal entries for adjusting entries a, d, and g.

Requirement 1

\	\			
\	\			

Journal

DATE	ACCOUNT TITLES AND EXPLANATIONS	POST REF.	DEBIT	CREDIT

Requirements 1 & 2

		Journal			
DATE		ACCOUNT TITLES AND EXPLANATIONS	POST REF.	DEBIT	CREDIT

P3-6A ③④⑤

Consider the unadjusted trial balance of Burrows Landscaping at December 31, 2020, and the related month-end adjustment data:

BURROWS LANDSCAPING		
Unadjusted Trial Balance		
December 31, 2020		
Cash	$ 34,500	
Accounts receivable	22,000	
Prepaid rent	9,000	
Supplies	5,500	
Equipment	66,000	
Accumulated amortization—equipment		$ 12,650
Accounts payable		7,200
Salaries payable		0
A. Burrows, capital		122,700
A. Burrows, withdrawals	25,000	
Landscaping design revenue		136,000
Salaries expense	82,000	
Rent expense	22,500	
Utilities expense	6,000	
Amortization expense—equipment	6,050	
Supplies expense	0	
Total	$278,550	$278,550

The following adjustments need to be made before the financial statements for the year can be prepared:

a. Accrued landscaping design revenue at December 31, $8,500.

b. One month of the prepaid rent had been used. The unadjusted prepaid balance of $9,000 is for a period of four months.

c. Supplies remaining on hand at December 31, $900.

d. Amortization on equipment for the month of December. The equipment's expected useful life is 10 years; it will have no value at the end of its useful life, and the straight-line method of amortization is used.

e. An accrual for two days of salaries is needed. The five-day weekly payroll is $10,000.

Required

1. Use the t-accounts on the next page to calculate the new balances. Prepare the adjusted trial balance of Burrows Landscaping at December 31, 2020.

2. Prepare the income statement (record expenses from largest to smallest on the income statement) and the statement of owner's equity for the year ended December 31, 2020, and the balance sheet at December 31, 2020. Draw the arrows linking the three financial statements.

Requirement 1

Cash	Accounts Receivable

Supplies	Prepaid Rent

Equipment	Accumulated Amortization—Equipment

Accounts Payable	Salaries Payable

Requirement 1 (Continued)

A. Burrows, Capital

A. Burrows, Withdrawals

Landscaping Design Revenue

Salaries Expense

Rent Expense

Utilities Expense

Amortization Expense-Equipment

Supplies Expense

Requirement 1 (Continued)

ACCOUNT	DEBIT	CREDIT

Calculations:

Requirement 2

Extra Journal Page

DATE	ACCOUNTS TITLES AND EXPLANATIONS	POST REF.	DEBIT	CREDIT

P3–7A ③ ④ ⑤

Online Security Buddies provides consulting services to small businesses that require computer security but are too small to have their own IT person on staff. The business had the following account balances:

ONLINE SECURITY BUDDIES		
Unadjusted Trial Balance		
December 1, 2020		
Account Title	**Debit**	**Credit**
Cash	$ 19,000	
Accounts receivable	23,200	
Supplies	5,000	
Prepaid advertising	1,500	
Computer equipment	69,000	
Accumulated amortization—computer equipment		$ 0
Server equipment	288,000	
Accumulated amortization—server equipment		0
Accounts payable		93,600
I. Steele, capital		186,000
I. Steele, withdrawals	79,000	
Consulting revenue		342,500
Salaries expense	120,000	
Supplies expense	0	
Utilities expense	17,400	
Total	$622,100	$622,100

The following transactions occurred during December:

a. On December 1, paid $11,500 cash to an advertising firm for four months of advertising work in advance.

b. On December 6, supplies in the amount of $3,700 were purchased on account.

c. On December 15, the company received a cash advance of $8,000 for work to be performed starting January 1, 2021.

d. On December 29, the company provided counselling services to a customer for $15,000, to be paid in 30 days.

The following information was available on December 31, 2020:

e. A physical count shows $7,600 of supplies remaining on hand on December 31.

f. The server equipment has an expected useful life of eight years with no expected value after eight years. The server equipment was purchased on January 2, and the straight-line method of amortization is used.

g. The computer equipment, purchased on January 2, is expected to be used for four years with no expected value after four years. The straight-line method of amortization is used.

h. The advertising firm has performed one-quarter of the work on the contract.

i. The company's senior consultant, who earns $800 per day, worked the last six days of the year and will be paid on January 4, 2018.

Required

1. Journalize the entries. Add new accounts if necessary.

2. Prepare an adjusted trial balance on December 31, 2020. List expenses in the order of dollar amount, from the greatest amount to the smallest.

3. Prepare an income statement for the year ended December 31, 2020. List expenses in the order of dollar amount, from the greatest amount to the smallest.

4. Prepare a statement of owner's equity for the year ended December 31, 2020. Assume there have been no changes to the capital account since January 1.
5. Prepare a balance sheet at December 31, 2020.

Requirement 1

Journal

DATE		ACCOUNT TITLES AND EXPLANATIONS	POST REF.	DEBIT	CREDIT

Optional

Requirement 2

ACCOUNT	DEBIT	CREDIT

Requirements 3 – 5

4 COMPLETING THE ACCOUNTING CYCLE

LEARNING OBJECTIVES

1 Prepare an accounting worksheet.
2 Complete the accounting cycle.
3 Close the revenue, expense, and withdrawal accounts.
4 Correct typical accounting errors.
5 Classify assets and liabilities as current or long-term, and prepare a classified balance sheet.
6 Use the current ratio and the debt ratio to evaluate a company.
7 Describe the accounting cycle and financial reporting implications of International Financial Reporting Standards (IFRS).

*A1 Describe and prepare reversing entries.

SOME USEFUL TEXT INFORMATION (add your own notes too)

EXHIBIT 4–7 | The Closing Process for Net Income

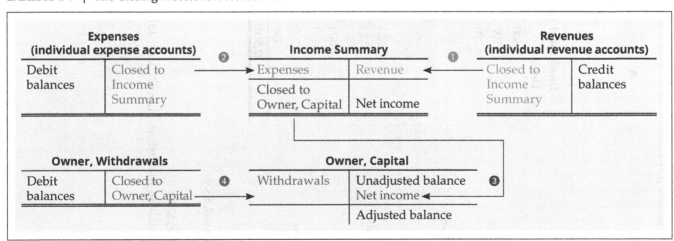

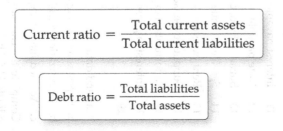

$$\text{Current ratio} = \frac{\text{Total current assets}}{\text{Total current liabilities}}$$

$$\text{Debt ratio} = \frac{\text{Total liabilities}}{\text{Total assets}}$$

S4-1 ①

Scissors Hair Stylists has begun the preparation of its adjusted trial balance as follows:

SCISSORS HAIR STYLISTS

Preparation of Adjusted Trial Balance

December 31, 2020

Account Title	Unadjusted Trial Balance		Adjustments		Adjusted Trial Balance	
	Debit	Credit	Debit	Credit	Debit	Credit
Cash	600					
Supplies	800					
Equipment	16,200					
Accumulated amortization—equipment		1,100				
Accounts payable		500				
Interest payable		0				
Note payable		2,900				
Suzanne Byrd, capital		5,300				
Service revenue		13,000				
Rent expense	4,800					
Supplies expense	0					
Amortization expense	0					
Interest expense	400					
	22,800	22,800				

Year-end data:

a. Supplies remaining on hand, $300

b. Amortization, $1,100

c. Accrued interest expense, $700

Complete the company's adjusted trial balance. Identify each adjustment by its letter. To save time, you may write your answer in the spaces provided on the adjusted trial balance.

S4-3 ①

A partial worksheet for Ramey Law Firm is presented below. Solve for the missing information.

	A	J	K	L	M
5		Income Statement		Balance Sheet	
6		Debit	Credit	Debit	Credit
32	Sub-total	(a)	$24,850	$211,325	$202,950
33	Net (b)	8,375			(c)
34	Total	(d)	$24,850	(e)	(f)
35					

S4-4 ①

A partial worksheet for Aaron Adjusters is presented below. Solve for the missing information.

	A	J	K	L	M
5		Income Statement		Balance Sheet	
6		Debit	Credit	Debit	Credit
32	Sub-total	$22,400	(a)	(b)	$61,400
33	Net (c)		5,300	(d)	
34	Total	(e)	(f)	(g)	$61,400
35					

S4-5 ① ②

Answer the following questions:

1. What type of balance does the Owner, Capital account have—debit or credit?

_____

2. Which income statement account has the same type of balance as the Capital account?

_____

3. Which type of income statement account has the opposite type of balance as the Capital account?

_____
_____
_____
_____

4. What do we call the difference between total debits and total credits on the income statement? Into what account is the difference figure closed at the end of the period?

_____
_____
_____
_____

S4–14 ④

Suppose a company made the following journal entry to pay for supplies purchased:

Mar. 31	Accounts Receivable	175	
	Cash		175
	To pay for supplies purchased on account.		

Is this an error? If so, correct the error using both methods shown in this chapter. Provide an explanation for each journal entry.

Journal				
DATE	ACCOUNT TITLES AND EXPLANATIONS	POST REF.	DEBIT	CREDIT

S4–16 ⑤

Indicate where each of the following accounts would be reported in the financial statements for the year ended December 31, 2019:

1. _____ Prepaid Rent
2. _____ Unearned Revenue
3. _____ Note Payable (due June 30, 2022)
4. _____ Accounts Receivable
5. _____ Accounts Payable
6. _____ Accumulated Amortization
7. _____ Supplies
8. _____ Company Truck

a. Property, plant, and equipment
b. Current asset
c. Current liability
d. Long-term liability

S4–19 ⑥

Garwood Racing has these account balances at December 31, 2020:

Accounts Payable	$ 8,700	Accum. Amortization—Equipment	$ 8,000
Accounts Receivable	12,500	Note Payable, Long-Term	18,000
Cash	6,500	Prepaid Rent	4,000
Supplies	3,000	Salaries Payable	4,200
Equipment	24,000	Service Revenue	62,000

Current ratio:

Debt ratio:

S4–21 ⑦

Answer the following questions about IFRS:

1. What are the two main options (those illustrated in the chapter) for balance sheet presentation for companies following IFRS?

2. Explain what is meant by the term "reverse order of liquidity."

3. What is another name for a balance sheet that may be used by corporations reporting under IFRS?

E4-2 ①

The unadjusted trial balance of Skydive Tours appears below:

	UNADJUSTED TRIAL BALANCE		ADJUSTMENTS	
SKYDIVE TOURS				
Worksheet				
September 30, 2020				
ACCOUNT TITLE	DEBIT	CREDIT	DEBIT	CREDIT
Cash	$14,240			
Accounts receivable	11,880			
Prepaid rent	2,400			
Supplies	6,780			
Equipment	65,200			
Accumulated amortization—equipment		$ 5,680		
Accounts payable		10,320		
Salaries payable		0		
R. Puri, capital		72,060		
R. Puri, withdrawals	6,000			
Service revenue		23,600		
Amortization expense—equipment	0			
Salaries expense	3,600			
Rent expense	0			
Utilities expense	1,560			
Supplies expense	0			
Total	$111,660	$111,660		

Additional information at September 30, 2020:

a. The business had corporate sales that were not recorded yet in the amount of $840. It must accrue this service revenue.

b. Equipment amortization in the amount of $260 needs to be recorded.

c. The business needs to accrue salaries expense of $2,100 for work done but not yet recorded.

d. Prepaid rent used in the amount of $1,200.

e. Supplies worth $3,200 were used up during the period.

Required Complete the Skydive Tours worksheet for September 2020. What was net income for the month ended September 30, 2020?

SKYDIVE TOURS					
Worksheet					
September 30, 2020					
ADJUSTED TRIAL BALANCE		INCOME STATEMENT		BALANCE SHEET	
DEBIT	CREDIT	DEBIT	CREDIT	DEBIT	CREDIT

E4-4 ③

Journalize the adjusting and closing entries for Skydive Tours' information shown in E4–2. Include explanations.

		Journal			
DATE		ACCOUNT TITLES AND EXPLANATIONS	POST REF.	DEBIT	CREDIT

E4–5 ③

Post the adjusting and closing entries from E4–4 to the accounts, identifying adjustment amounts as *Adj.*, closing amounts as *Clo.*, and balances as *Bal.* Double underline the accounts with zero balances after you close them and show the ending balance in each account.

Accounts Receivable		
Bal.	11,880	

Prepaid Rent		
Bal.	2,400	

Supplies		
Bal.	6,780	

Accumulated Amortization—Equipment		
	Bal.	5,680

Salaries Payable		

R. Puri, Capital		
	Bal.	72,060

R. Puri, Withdrawals		
Bal.	6,000	

Income Summary		

Service Revenue		
	Bal.	23,600

Amortization Expense—Equipment		

Salaries Expense		
Bal.	3,600	

Rent Expense		

Supplies Expense		

Utilities Expense		
Bal.	1,560	

E4–9 ③

The adjusted trial balance for Pria's Music Lessons follows:

PRIA'S MUSIC LESSONS		
Adjusted Trial Balance		
December 31, 2020		
Cash	$ 27,600	
Supplies	7,500	
Prepaid rent	3,600	
Instruments	168,900	
Accumulated amortization—instruments		$ 26,050
Accounts payable		29,300
Salaries payable		3,250
Unearned service revenue		17,600
P. Chai, capital		153,300
P. Chai, withdrawals	15,000	
Service revenue		61,000
Salaries expense	45,200	
Rent expense	15,650	
Amortization expense—instruments	1,200	
Supplies expense	2,650	
Utilities expense	3,200	
	$290,500	$290,500

Required

1. Journalize the closing entries of Pria's Music Lessons at December 31, 2020. Include explanations.
2. How much net income or net loss did Pria's Music Lessons earn for the period ended December 31, 2020? How can you tell?

Requirement 1

		Journal			
DATE		ACCOUNT TITLES AND EXPLANATIONS	POST REF.	DEBIT	CREDIT

Requirement 2

132 Chapter 4

E4-12 ④

Prepare a correcting entry (or entries), with explanations, for each of the following accounting errors:

Nov. 3   Debited Supplies and credited Accounts Payable for a $9,000 purchase of office equipment on account.
Nov. 6   Accrued interest revenue of $3,000 by a debit to Accounts Receivable and a credit to Interest Revenue.
Nov. 8   Adjusted prepaid rent by debiting Prepaid Rent and crediting Rent Expense for $4,000. This adjusting entry should have debited Rent Expense and credited Prepaid Rent for $4,000.
Nov. 12   Debited Salaries Expense and credited Accounts Payable to accrue salaries expense of $12,000.
Nov. 19   Recorded the earning of $7,800 service revenue collected in advance by debiting Accounts Receivable and crediting Service Revenue.

Journal				
DATE	ACCOUNT TITLES AND EXPLANATIONS	POST REF.	DEBIT	CREDIT

Journal

DATE	ACCOUNT TITLES AND EXPLANATIONS	POST REF.	DEBIT	CREDIT

*E4–17 Ⓐ①

On December 31, 2020, Rexall Industries recorded an adjusting entry for $10,000 of accrued interest revenue. On January 15, 2021, the company received interest payments in the amount of $22,000. Assuming Rexall Industries uses reversing entries, prepare the 2020 and 2021 journal entries for these interest transactions.

Journal

DATE	ACCOUNT TITLES AND EXPLANATIONS	POST REF.	DEBIT	CREDIT

E4-19 ①

This exercise continues recordkeeping for the Canyon Canoe Company from previous chapters.

Required Complete the worksheet at December 31, 2020. Use the unadjusted trial balance from Chapter 2 and the adjusting entries from Chapter 3. If you have not completed them, you can still answer this question with the following information:

CANYON CANOE COMPANY				
Worksheet				
December 31, 2020				
	UNADJUSTED TRIAL BALANCE		ADJUSTMENTS	
ACCOUNT TITLE	DEBIT	CREDIT	DEBIT	CREDIT
Cash	$ 12,125			
Accounts receivable	5,750			
Office supplies	1,250			
Prepaid rent	3,000			
Land	85,000			
Building	35,000			
Canoes	12,000			
Accounts payable		$ 3,670		
Unearned revenue		750		
Note payable		7,200		
Amber Wilson, capital		136,000		
Amber Wilson, withdrawals	450			
Canoe rental revenue		12,400		
Rent expense	1,200			
Salaries expense	3,300			
Utilities expense	445			
Telephone expense	500			
Total	$160,020	$160,020		

At December 31, the business gathers the following information for the adjusting entries:

a. At December 31, the office supplies on hand totaled $165.

b. Prepaid rent of one month has been used. (Hint: Total is for three months.)

c. Determine the amortization on the building using straight-line amortization. Assume the useful life of the building is five years and the residual value is $5,000. (Hint: The building was purchased on December 1.)

CANYON CANOE COMPANY					
Worksheet					
December 31, 2020					
ADJUSTED TRIAL BALANCE		INCOME STATEMENT		BALANCE SHEET	
DEBIT	CREDIT	DEBIT	CREDIT	DEBIT	CREDIT

d. $400 of unearned revenue has now been earned.

e. The employee who has been working the rental booth has earned $1,250 in salaries that will be paid January 15, 2021.

f. Canyon Canoe Company has earned $1,850 of canoe rental revenue that has not been recorded or received.

g. Determine the amortization on the canoes purchased on November 3 using the straight-line method. Assume the useful life of the canoes is four years and the residual value is $0.

h. Determine the amortization on the canoes purchased on December 2 using the straight-line amortization method. Assume the useful life of the canoes is four years and the residual value is $0.

i. Interest expense of $50 has accrued on the note payable.

E4-20 ② ③ ⑤

This exercise continues recordkeeping for the Canyon Canoe Company. If you did not complete those exercises, or E4-19 then you can use the following information at this time:

ACCOUNT TITLE	DEBIT	CREDIT
CANYON CANOE COMPANY		
Adjusted Trial Balance		
December 31, 2020		
Cash	$ 12,125	
Accounts receivable	7,600	
Office supplies	165	
Prepaid rent	2,000	
Land	85,000	
Building	35,000	
Accumulated amortization—building		$ 500
Canoes	12,000	
Accumulated amortization—canoes		350
Accounts payable		3,670
Unearned revenue		350
Salaries payable		1,250
Interest payable		50
Note payable		7,200
Amber Wilson, capital		136,000
Amber Wilson, withdrawals	450	
Canoe rental revenue		14,650
Rent expense	2,200	
Salaries expense	4,550	
Utilities expense	445	
Telephone expense	500	
Supplies expense	1,085	
Amortization expense—building	500	
Amortization expense—canoes	350	
Interest expense	50	
Total	$ 164,020	$ 164,020

Required

1. Prepare an income statement for the two months ended December 31, 2020.
2. Prepare a statement of owner's equity for the two months ended December 31, 2020.
3. Prepare a classified balance sheet (report form) at December 31, 2020. Assume the note payable is long-term.
4. Journalize the closing entries at December 31, 2020.
5. Open T-accounts for Income Summary and Amber Wilson, Capital. Post the entries from requirement 3 and determine the ending balance for both accounts. Denote each closing amount as *Clos.* and each account balance as *Bal.*
6. Prepare a post-closing trial balance at December 31, 2020.

Requirements 1 and 2

Requirement 3

Requirement 4

		Journal			
DATE		ACCOUNT TITLES AND EXPLANATIONS	POST REF.	DEBIT	CREDIT

Requirement 5

Income Summary	Amber Wilson, Capital

Requirement 6

CANYON CANOE COMPANY		
Post-Closing Trial Balance		
December 31, 2020		
ACCOUNT	DEBIT	CREDIT
Cash		
Accounts receivable		
Office Supplies		
Prepaid rent		
Land		
Building		
Accumulated amortization-building		
Canoes		
Accumulated amortization-canoes		
Accounts payable		
Unearned revenue		
Salaries payable		
Interest payable		
Note payable		
Amber Wilson, capital		
Total		

	Extra Journal Paper			
DATE	ACCOUNTS TITLES AND EXPLANATIONS	POST REF.	DEBIT	CREDIT

P4–1A ①

The unadjusted trial balance of Dorset Roofing at July 31, 2020, appears below:

	UNDAJUSTED TRIAL BALANCE		ADJUSTMENTS	
ACCOUNT TITLE	DEBIT	CREDIT	DEBIT	CREDIT
Cash	127,200			
Accounts receivable	226,920			
Supplies	105,960			
Prepaid insurance	23,800			
Equipment	196,140			
Accum. amort.—equip.		157,440		
Building	257,340			
Accum. amort.—building		63,000		
Land	179,800			
Accounts payable		136,140		
Interest payable		0		
Wages payable		0		
Unearned service revenue		63,360		
Notes payable, long-term		134,400		
T. Jackson, capital		474,780		
T. Jackson, withdrawals	25,200			
Service revenue		141,140		
Amort. expense—equip.	0			
Amort. expense—bldg.	0			
Wages expense	19,200			
Insurance expense	0			
Interest expense	0			
Utilities expense	6,660			
Advertising expense	2,040			
Supplies expense	0			
	1,170,260	1,170,260		

DORSET ROOFING / Worksheet / July 31, 2020

Additional data at July 31, 2020:

a. Amortization for the period to be recorded: equipment, $2,040; building, $4,210.

b. Wages expense to be recorded because employees worked but have not yet been paid, $3,440.

c. A count of supplies showed that unused supplies amounted to $88,440.

d. During July, $5,000 of prepaid insurance coverage was used.

e. Accrued interest expense, $2,080.

DORSET ROOFING					
Worksheet					
July 31, 2020					
ADJUSTED TRIAL BALANCE		INCOME STATEMENT		BALANCE SHEET	
DEBIT	CREDIT	DEBIT	CREDIT	DEBIT	CREDIT

f. Of the $63,360 balance of Unearned Service Revenue, $29,820 was earned during July.

g. Accrued advertising expense, $2,600 (credit Accounts Payable).

h. The company performed $9,600 of services for a client and has not yet been paid.

Required   Complete Dorset Roofing's worksheet for July. Identify each adjusting entry by its letter.

P4–6A ② ③ ⑤ ⑥

The *adjusted* trial balance of Coastal Creations at June 30, 2020, the end of the company's fiscal year, appears below.

Required

1. Prepare the income statement and statement of owner's equity for the year ended June 30, 2020, and the classified balance sheet on that date. Use the account format for the balance sheet. Report expenses from largest to smallest amount.

2. Journalize the closing entries.

3. Compute Coastal Creations' current ratio and debt ratio at June 30, 2020. One year ago the current ratio stood at 1.81 and the debt ratio was 0.71. Did Coastal Creations' ability to pay debts improve or deteriorate during the fiscal year?

COASTAL CREATIONS		
Adjusted Trial Balance		
June 30, 2020		
Cash	$ 12,610	
Accounts receivable	15,882	
Supplies	18,774	
Prepaid insurance	1,920	
Equipment	33,480	
Accumulated amortization—equipment		$ 9,888
Building	68,940	
Accumulated amortization—building		10,110
Land	18,000	
Accounts payable		25,040
Interest payable		1,894
Salaries payable		1,462
Unearned service revenue		1,380
Note payable, long-term		58,200
A. Kapoor, capital		41,034
A. Kapoor, withdrawals	28,180	
Service revenue		83,916
Amortization expense—equipment	4,380	
Amortization expense—building	2,382	
Salaries expense	13,882	
Insurance expense	1,860	
Interest expense	7,906	
Utilities expense	2,580	
Supplies expense	2,148	
Total	$232,924	$232,924

Requirement 1

Requirement 1 (Continued)

Note: If needed, create a second dollar-column for assets.

Requirement 2

	Journal				
DATE	ACCOUNT TITLES AND EXPLANATIONS	POST REF.	DEBIT	CREDIT	

Requirement 3

Current ratio:

Debt ratio:

_____

_____

_____

_____

_____

_____

_____

P4–7A ⑤ ⑥

The accounts of Bolton Travel at December 31, 2020, are listed below in alphabetical order:

Accounts Payable	$ 15,300		Interest Payable	$ 4,300
Accounts Receivable	19,800		Interest Receivable	1,600
Accumulated			Land	62,500
Amortization—Building	113,400		Note Payable, Long-Term	91,400
Accumulated Amortization—			Note Receivable,	
Furniture	34,800		Long-Term	12,500
Advertising Expense	6,600		Intangible Assets	9,300
Amortization Expense	3,900		Other Current Liabilities	14,100
Building	313,200		Prepaid Insurance	3,300
Cash	25,000		Prepaid Rent	12,700
Commission Revenue	280,500		Salaries Expense	73,800
E. Bolton, Capital	209,400		Salaries Payable	6,700
E. Bolton, Withdrawals	143,800		Supplies	8,500
Furniture	68,100		Supplies Expense	17,100
Insurance Expense	2,400		Unearned Commission	
			Revenue	14,200

Required

1. Prepare the company's classified balance sheet in report format at December 31, 2020. Use a three-column format for the amounts. *All adjustments have been journalized and posted, but the closing entries have not yet been made.*

2. Compute Bolton Travel's current ratio and debt ratio at December 31, 2020. At December 31, 2019, the current ratio was 1.52 and the debt ratio was 0.20. Did Bolton Travel's ability to pay both current and total debts improve or deteriorate during 2020?

Requirement 1

Requirement 2

Current ratio:

Debt ratio:

_____

_____

_____

_____

_____

_____

_____

_____

_____

_____

_____

5 MERCHANDISING OPERATIONS

LEARNING OBJECTIVES

1 Describe merchandising operations.
2 Account for the purchase and sale of inventory under the perpetual inventory system.
3 Adjust and close the accounts of a merchandising business under the perpetual inventory system.
4 Prepare a merchandiser's financial statements under the perpetual inventory system.
5 Use the gross margin percentage and the inventory turnover ratio to evaluate a business.
6 Describe the merchandising operations effects of International Financial Reporting Standards (IFRS).

*A1 Account for the purchase and sale of inventory under the periodic system.
*A2 Compute the cost of goods sold under the periodic inventory system.
*A3 Adjust and close the accounts of a merchandising business under the periodic inventory system.
*A4 Prepare a merchandiser's financial statements under the periodic inventory system.
*B1 Compare the perpetual and periodic inventory systems.

SOME USEFUL TEXT INFORMATION (add your own notes too)

EXHIBIT 5–7 | Summary of Activities Affecting the Inventory and Cost of Goods Sold Accounts

Inventory			
Dec. 31, 2019, balance	XXX	XXX	Purchase discounts during 2020
Purchases of merchandise during 2020	XXX	XXX	Purchases returns and allowances during 2020
Freight-in costs incurred during 2020	XXX	421,000	Cost of sales transactions during 2020
Return of goods to inventory	XXX		Adjustment for shrinkage shrinkage after physical count
		6,000	
Dec. 31, 2020, balance	168,000		

Cost of Goods Sold			
Cost of sales for 2020	421,000	XXX	Return of goods to inventory
Adjustment for shrinkage after physical count	6,000		
Dec. 31, 2020, balance	427,000		

EXHIBIT 5–9 | Merchandiser Multi-Step Income Statement

SLOPES SKI SHOP
Income Statement
For the Year Ended December 31, 2020

Sales revenue		$777,000
Less: Sales discounts	$7,500	
Sales returns and allowances	8,000	15,500
Net sales revenue		761,500
Cost of goods sold		427,000
Gross margin		334,500
Operating expenses		201,000
Selling expenses	126,000	
General expenses	75,000	
Income from operations		133,500
Other revenue and expense		
Interest revenue	3,000	
Less: Interest expense	4,500	(1,500)
Net income		$132,000

> These are activities outside the scope of selling merchandise.

Sales revenue − Sales discounts − Sales returns and allowances = Net sales revenue

$$\text{Gross margin percentage} = \frac{\text{Gross margin}}{\text{Net sales revenue}}$$

$$\text{Inventory turnover} = \frac{\text{Cost of goods sold}}{\text{Average inventory}} = \frac{\text{Cost of goods sold}}{\dfrac{\text{Beginning inventory} + \text{Ending inventory}}{2}}$$

$$\text{Inventory turnover in days} = \frac{365}{\text{inventory turnover}}$$

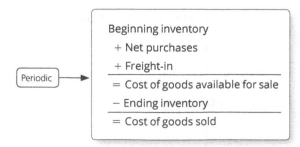

Periodic →

Beginning inventory
+ Net purchases
+ Freight-in
= Cost of goods available for sale
− Ending inventory
= Cost of goods sold

S5–1 (1)

Match the accounting terminology to the definitions.

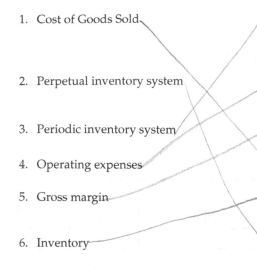

1. Cost of Goods Sold

2. Perpetual inventory system

3. Periodic inventory system

4. Operating expenses

5. Gross margin

6. Inventory

a. An inventory system that requires businesses to obtain a physical count of inventory to determine quantities on hand.

b. Expenses, other than Cost of Goods Sold, that are incurred in the entity's major ongoing operations.

c. Excess of Sales Revenue over Cost of Goods Sold.

d. The cost of inventory that the business has sold to customers.

e. Goods the company owns and expects to sell to customers in the normal course of operations.

f. An inventory system that keeps a running record of inventory.

S5–7 (2)

Details of purchase invoices, including shipping terms, credit terms, and returns, appear below. Compute the total amount to be paid in full settlement of each invoice, assuming that credit for returns is granted before the expiration of the discount period and payment is made within the discount period. (Hint: Assume FOB destination freight is included in the invoice price.)

Invoice	Freight and Credit Terms	Transportation Charges	Returns and Allowances
a. $2,000	FOB destination, 3/10, n/45	$ 55	$200
b. $5,500	FOB shipping point, 2/10, n/30	$100	$ 50
c. $6,700	FOB shipping point, 2/10, n/45	$200	$350
d. $9,300	FOB destination, 2/10, n/60	$150	$550

(a) $2000 - 200 = 1800. \rightarrow 1800 (1 - 0.03) = \$1746$

(b) $5500 - 50 = 5450 (1 - 0.02) \ \$5341 + 100 = \$5441$
* Shipping cost is not part of the discount.

(c) $6700 - 350 = 6350 (1 - 0.02) = 6223 + 200 = \$6423$

(d) $9300 - 550 = 8750 (1 - 0.02) = \$8575.$

S5-8 ②

Consider the following transactions for Burlington Drug Store:

Feb. 2   Burlington buys $23,800 worth of inventory on account with credit terms of 2/15, n/30, FOB shipping point.
     4   Burlington pays a $50 freight charge.
     9   Burlington returns $5,200 of the merchandise due to damage during shipment.
     14   Burlington pays the amount due, less return and discount.

Required

1. Journalize the purchase transactions. Explanations are not required.
2. In the final analysis, how much did the inventory cost Burlington Drug Store?

	Journal			
DATE	ACCOUNT TITLES AND EXPLANATIONS	POST REF.	DEBIT	CREDIT

S5-9 ②

Spanner Inc. sells $160,000 of women's sportswear to Lululime under credit terms of 2/10, net 30 on August 1, 2020. Spanner's cost of the goods is $76,000, and Spanner receives the appropriate amount of cash from Lululime on August 10, 2020. Assume Spanner Inc. uses the perpetual inventory system.

Journalize Spanner's transactions for August 1, 2020, and August 10, 2020.

\multicolumn{6}{c}{Journal}
DATE		ACCOUNT TITLES AND EXPLANATIONS	POST REF.	DEBIT	CREDIT

S5–10 ②

Journalize the following sales transactions for Salem Sportswear. Explanations are not required.

Jul. 1 Salem sold $20,000 of men's sportswear for cash. Cost of goods sold is $10,000.

3 Salem sold $62,000 of women's sportswear on account, credit terms are 3/10, n/30. Cost of goods is $31,000.

5 Salem received a $4,500 sales return on damaged goods from the customer on July 1. Cost of goods damaged is $2,250. Money was refunded.

10 Salem receives payment from the customer on the amount due, less discount.

		Journal			
DATE		ACCOUNT TITLES AND EXPLANATIONS	POST REF.	DEBIT	CREDIT

S5–11 ③

Beachcombers Inc.'s Inventory account at January 31 showed a debit balance of $150,000. A physical count of inventory showed goods on hand of $147,000. Journalize the adjusting entry. Beachcombers uses the perpetual inventory system.

Journal					
DATE		ACCOUNT TITLES AND EXPLANATIONS	POST REF.	DEBIT	CREDIT

S5–13 ④

Suppose Dawson Communications uses the perpetual inventory system and reported these figures in its December 31, 2020, financial statements:

Accounts payable	$118,000
Accounts receivable	5,600
Accrued liabilities	3,200
Cash	7,600
Cost of goods sold	40,000
Equipment, net	17,400
Inventory	800
Long-term notes payable	1,800
Net sales revenue	100,000
Total operating expenses	37,000
V. Dawson, capital	18,400

Prepare Dawson Communications' multi-step income statement for the year ended December 31, 2020.

Net Sales Revenue		100 000
Less		
Cost of Goods		40 000
GROSS Propit		60 000
(—) Operating Expenses		(37 000)
Net Income,		23 000

S5-14 ④

Use the data in S5-13 to prepare Dawson Communications' classified balance sheet at December 31, 2020. Use the report format with all headings.

S5-18 ⑥

What are two key criteria that merchandisers who report under IFRS must follow? Do these criteria differ from those followed by companies that report under ASPE?

E5–3 ②

Suppose The Bay uses the perpetual inventory system and purchases $300,000 of sporting goods on account from Nike on April 10, 2020. Credit terms are 1/10, net 30. The Bay pays electronically on April 20, 2002, and Nike receives the money the same day.

Journalize The Bay's (a) purchase and (b) cash payment transactions. What was The Bay's net cost of this inventory?

Note: E5–4 covers this same situation for the seller.

DATE		ACCOUNT TITLES AND EXPLANATIONS	POST REF.	DEBIT	CREDIT
April	10	Inventory		300 000	
		Accounts Payable			300 000
April	20	Accounts Payable		300 000	
		Cash			297000
		Inventory			3000

Net cost of Inventory:

E5–4 ②

Nike uses the perpetual inventory system and sells $300,000 of sporting goods to The Bay under credit terms of 1/10, net 30 on April 10, 2020. Nike's cost of the goods is $210,000, and it receives the appropriate amount of cash from The Bay on April 20, 2020.

Journalize Nike's transactions on April 10, 2020, and April 20, 2020. How much gross margin did Nike earn on this sale?

DATE		ACCOUNT TITLES AND EXPLANATIONS	POST REF.	DEBIT	CREDIT
April	10	Accounts Receivable		300 000	
		Sales Revenue			300 000
April	10	Cost of Goods Sold		210 000	
		Inventory			210 000
April	20	Cash		297 000	
		Sales discount		3 000	
		Accounts receivable			300 000

Gross Margin:

E5–6 ②

On April 30, 2020, Ladysmith Jewellers purchased inventory of $90,000 on account from Northern Gems Ltd., a jewellery importer. Terms were 2/15, n/45. On receiving the goods, Ladysmith checked the order and found $5,500 worth of items that were not ordered but included in the invoice. Therefore, Ladysmith returned this amount of merchandise to Northern on May 4. On May 14, Ladysmith paid Northern.

Required

1. Journalize all necessary transactions for Ladysmith Jewellers, which uses the perpetual inventory system. Explanations are not required.
2. Journalize the transactions of Northern Gems Ltd., which uses the perpetual inventory system. Northern's gross margin is 35 percent, so cost of goods sold is 65 percent of sales. Explanations are not required.

Journal

DATE	ACCOUNT TITLES AND EXPLANATIONS	POST REF.	DEBIT	CREDIT
Apr 30	Inventory		90 000	
	Accounts Payable			90 000
May 4	A/P		5500	
	Inv.			5500
May 14	A/P		84500	
	Cash			82810
	Inv.			1690
Apr 30	A/c Receivable		90 000	
	Sales Revenue			90000
	COGS (65% of sales)		58 500	
	Inventory			58 500
May 4	Sales Return		5500	
	A/c Receivable			5500
	Inventory		3575	
	COGS			3575
May 14	Cash		82 810	
	Sales discount			1690
	Acc Receivable			84 500

E5–8 ②

Supply the missing income statement amounts in each of the following situations:

Sales	Sales Discounts	Net Sales	Cost of Goods Sold	Gross Margin
$94,500	$2,200	$92,300	$56,700	(a) _____
99,500	(b) _____	95,520	(c) _____	$36,000
68,700	2,100	(d) _____	37,700	(e) _____
(f) _____	3,500	(g) _____	52,500	18,600

Calculations:

E5–11 ③

Bubble Tea's accounts at December 31, 2020, included these unadjusted balances:

Inventory	$ 4,400
Cost of Goods Sold..	31,200
Sales Revenue	46,800
Sales Discounts	1,250
Sales Returns and Allowances	700

The physical count of inventory showed $3,700 of inventory on hand. This is the only adjustment needed.

Required

1. Journalize the adjustment for inventory shrinkage. Include an explanation. Bubble Tea uses the perpetual inventory system.
2. Journalize the closing entries for the appropriate accounts.
3. Compute the gross margin.

Requirements 1 & 2

Journal					
DATE	ACCOUNT TITLES AND EXPLANATIONS	POST REF.	DEBIT	CREDIT	

Requirement 3 — Gross Margin

_____
_____
_____
_____
_____
_____
_____

E5–14 (4)

Bark Buddy reported the following figures from its adjusted trial balance for its first year of business, which ended on July 31, 2020:

Cash	$2,900	Cost of Goods Sold	$18,700
Selling Expenses	1,400	Equipment, Net	9,500
Accounts Payable	4,300	Accrued Liabilities	1,800
C. Camilia, Capital	4,365	Net Sales Revenue	29,200
Notes Payable, Long-Term	500	Accounts Receivable	3,200
Inventory	1,100	Interest Expense	65
Administrative Expenses	3,300		

Prepare Bark Buddy's multi-step income statement for the year ended July 31, 2020.

*E5–17 Ⓐ⑴

Journalize, without explanations, the following transactions of Digbey Auto Parts, a distributor that uses the periodic inventory system, during the month of June 2020:

Jun. 3 Purchased $16,800 of inventory under terms of 2/10, n/eom and FOB shipping point.

7 Returned $1,600 of defective merchandise purchased on June 3.

9 Paid freight bill of $350 on June 3 purchase.

10 Sold inventory for $22,400, collecting cash of $3,600. Payment terms on the remainder were 2/15, n/30.

12 Paid amount owed on credit purchase of June 3.

16 Granted a sales allowance of $1,200 on the June 10 sale.

23 Received cash from the June 10 customer in full settlement of the debt.

	Journal				
DATE	ACCOUNT TITLES AND EXPLANATIONS		POST REF.	DEBIT	CREDIT

*E5–23   Ⓐ2

Rees Distributors uses the periodic inventory system. Rees reported these amounts at May 31, 2020:

Inventory, May 31, 2019	$29,000
Inventory, May 31, 2020	31,000
Purchases (of inventory)	82,000
Purchase Discounts	2,000
Purchase Returns	3,000
Freight-in	4,000
Sales Revenue	200,000
Sales Discounts	13,000
Sales Returns	15,000

Compute Rees Distributors':

a. Net sales revenue

b. Cost of goods sold

c. Gross margin

a. – c.

	Extra Journal Page			
DATE	ACCOUNT TITLES AND EXPLANATIONS	POST REF.	DEBIT	CREDIT

E5-25 ②

This exercise continues recordkeeping for the Canyon Canoe Company. At the beginning of the new year, Canyon Canoe Company decided to carry and sell T-shirts with its logo printed on them. Canyon Canoe Company uses the perpetual inventory system to account for the inventory. During January 2021, Canyon Canoe Company completed the following merchandising transactions:

Jan.	1	Purchased 10 T-shirts at $4 each and paid cash.
	2	Sold 6 T-shirts for $10 each, total cost of $24. Received cash.
	3	Purchased 50 T-shirts on account at $5 each. Terms 2/10, n/30.
	7	Paid the supplier for the T-shirts purchased on January 3, less discount.
	8	Realized 4 T-shirts from the January 1 order were printed incorrectly and returned them for a cash refund.
	10	Sold 40 T-shirts on account for $10 each, total cost of $200. Terms 3/15, n/45.
	12	Received payment for the T-shirts sold on account on January 10, less discount.
	14	Purchased 100 T-shirts on account at $4 each. Terms 4/15, n/30.
	18	Canyon Canoe Company contacted the supplier from the January 14 purchase and told it that some of the T-shirts were the wrong color. The supplier offered a $50 purchase allowance.
	20	Paid the supplier for the T-shirts purchased on January 14, less the allowance and discount.
	21	Sold 60 T-shirts on account for $10 each, total cost of $220. Terms 2/20, n/30.
	23	Received a payment on account for the T-shirts sold on January 21, less discount.
	25	Purchased 320 T-shirts on account at $5 each. Terms 2/10, n/30, FOB shipping point.
	27	Paid freight associated with the January 25 purchase, $48.
	29	Paid for the January 25 purchase, less discount.
	30	Sold 275 T-shirts on account for $10 each, total cost of $1,300. Terms 2/10, n/30.
	31	Received payment for the T-shirts sold on January 30, less discount.

Required

1. T-accounts from chapter 4 are included here to get you started.
2. Journalize and post the January transactions. Compute each account balance, and denote the balance as *Bal.* Explanations are not required.

Journal				
DATE	ACCOUNT TITLES AND EXPLANATIONS	POST REF.	DEBIT	CREDIT

Journal

DATE		ACCOUNT TITLES AND EXPLANATIONS	POST REF.	DEBIT	CREDIT

Journal

DATE		ACCOUNT TITLES AND EXPLANATIONS	POST REF.	DEBIT	CREDIT

Requirement 2

Cash	
Bal. 12,125	

Accounts Receivable	
Bal. 7,600	

Inventory	
Bal 0	

Office Supplies	
Bal. 165	

Prepaid Rent	
Bal. 2,000	

Land	
Bal. 85,000	

Building	
Bal. 35,000	

Accumulated Amortization— Building	
	Bal. 500

Canoes	
Bal. 12,000	

Accumulated Amortization— Canoes	
	Bal. 350

Accounts Payable	
	Bal. 3,670

Salaries Payable	
	Bal. 1,250

Interest Payable	
	Bal. 50

Unearned Revenue	
	Bal. 350

Note Payable	
	Bal. 7,200

Amber Wilson, Capital	
	Bal. 140,520

Income Summary	

Sales Revenue	

Requirement 2 (Continued)

| Sales Discounts | Canoe Rental Revenue | Cost of Goods Sold |

| Rent Expense | Salaries Expense | Utilities Expense |

| Telephone Expense | Supplies Expense | Amortization Expense— Building |

| Amortization Expense— Canoes | Interest Expense |

P5–2A ②

The following transactions occurred between Happy Pharmaceuticals and Zari Drug Store during February. Both companies use the perpetual inventory system.

Feb. 6   Zari purchased $60,000 of merchandise from Happy on credit terms of 1/10, n/30, FOB shipping point. Separately, Zari paid a $1,000 bill for freight-in. Happy invoiced Zari for $60,000 (these goods cost Happy $36,000).

10   Zari returned $5,000 of the merchandise purchased on February 6. Happy issued a credit memo for this amount and returned the goods to inventory (cost, $3,000).

15   Zari paid $24,000 of the invoice amount owed to Happy for the February 6 purchase. Happy allows its customers to take the cash discount on partial payments.

27   Zari paid the remaining amount owed to Happy for the February 6 purchase.

Required   Journalize these transactions, first on the books of Zari Drug Store and second on the books of Happy Pharmaceuticals.

Journal

DATE		ACCOUNT TITLES AND EXPLANATIONS	POST REF.	DEBIT	CREDIT

P5-3A ②

Singh Distributing Company uses the perpetual inventory system and engaged in the following transactions during May of the current year:

May	3	Purchased office supplies for cash, $22,000.
	7	Purchased inventory on credit terms of 3/10, net eom, $76,000.
	8	Returned 25 percent of the inventory purchased on May 7. It was not the inventory ordered.
	10	Sold goods for cash, $34,000 (cost, $20,400).
	13	Sold inventory on credit terms of 2/15, n/45 for $148,200, less $13,500 quantity discount offered to customers who purchase in large quantities (cost, $90,480).
	16	Paid the amount owed on account from the purchase of May 7, less the discount and the return.
	17	Received wrong-sized inventory as a sales return from May 13 sale, $12,400, which is the net amount after the quantity discount. Singh's cost of the inventory received was $7,440.
	18	Purchased inventory of $164,000 on account. Payment terms were 2/10, net 30.
	26	Paid supplier for goods purchased on May 18.
	28	Received cash in full settlement of the account from the customer who purchased inventory on May 13.
	31	Purchased inventory for cash, $96,000, less a quantity discount of $9,600, plus freight charges of $2,200.

Required

1. Journalize the preceding transactions on the books of Singh Distributing Company.
2. Suppose the balance in Inventory was $60,000 on May 1. What is the balance in inventory on May 31?

Requirement 1

	Journal			
DATE	ACCOUNT TITLES AND EXPLANATIONS	POST REF.	DEBIT	CREDIT

Requirement 1 (Continued)

		Journal			
DATE		ACCOUNT TITLES AND EXPLANATIONS	POST REF.	DEBIT	CREDIT

Requirement 2

Inventory

P5–5A ③ ④

Buono Adventures, which uses the perpetual inventory system, has the following account balances (in alphabetical order) on July 31, 2020:

Accounts Payable	$	21,600
Accounts Receivable		23,200
Accumulated Amortization—Equipment		64,600
Cash		8,400
Cost of Goods Sold		687,000
E. Buono, Capital		402,000
E. Buono, Withdrawals		92,000
Equipment		180,000
Interest Earned		4,000
Inventory		143,000
Operating Expenses		355,000
Sales Discounts		10,300
Sales Returns and Allowances		32,900
Sales Revenue		1,045,200
Supplies		14,600
Unearned Sales Revenue		9,000

Note: For simplicity, all operating expenses have been summarized in the account Operating Expenses.

Additional data at July 31, 2020:

a. A physical count of items showed $3,000 of supplies on hand. (*Hint:* Use the account Operating Expenses in the adjusting journal entry.)

b. An inventory count showed inventory on hand at July 31, 2020, of $140,000.

c. The equipment has an estimated useful life of eight years and is expected to have no scrap or residual value at the end of its life. (*Hint:* Use the account Operating Expenses in the adjusting journal entry.)

d. Unearned sales revenue of $5,600 was earned by July 31, 2020.

Required

1. Record all adjustments and closing entries that would be required on July 31, 2020.

2. Prepare the multi-step income statement and statement of owner's equity for the year ended July 31, 2020, and the classified balance sheet in report format as at July 31, 2020.

Requirement 1

		Journal			
DATE		ACCOUNT TITLES AND EXPLANATIONS	POST REF.	DEBIT	CREDIT

Requirement 2

Requirement 2 (Continued)

P5-6A ④

Items from the accounts of Marchand Distributors at May 31, 2020, follow, listed in alphabetical order. Marchand Distributors uses the perpetual inventory system. For simplicity, the operating expenses are summarized in the General Expenses and the Selling Expenses accounts.

Accounts Payable	$ 51,000	Interest Payable	$ 2,800
Accounts Receivable	107,500	Interest Revenue	600
Accumulated Amortization—Equipment	96,900	Inventory, May 31, 2020	147,100
C. Marchand, Capital	167,800	Notes Payable, Long-Term	114,800
C. Marchand, Withdrawals	66,900	Salaries Payable	7,200
Cash	19,900	Sales Discounts	26,500
Cost of Goods Sold	1,086,900	Sales Returns and Allowances	45,900
Equipment	340,800	Sales Revenue	1,991,500
General Expenses	206,800	Selling Expenses	357,200
Interest Expense	9,200	Supplies	33,100
		Unearned Sales Revenue	15,200

Required

1. Prepare the business's single-step income statement for the year ended May 31, 2020. Show Net Sales Revenue and not the individual accounts.

2. Prepare the statement of owner's equity for the year ended May 31, 2020.

3. Prepare Marchand Distributors' classified balance sheet in report format at May 31, 2020.

Requirement 1

Requirement 2

Requirement 3

P5–7A ④ ⑤

1. Use the data in P5–6A to prepare Marchand Distributors' multi-step income statement for the year ended May 31, 2020.
2. Corry Marchand, owner of the company, strives to earn a gross margin of at least 50 percent and a net income of 20 percent (Net income percentage = Net income ÷ Net sales revenue). Did Marchand Distributors achieve these goals? Show your calculations. Round these answers to one decimal place.

Requirement 1

Requirement 2

Gross margin   =
   percentage

Net income   =
   percentage

*P5-12A (A3)

The unadjusted trial balance of Marvin's Fine Gems at December 31, 2020, is shown below:

MARVIN'S FINE GEMS		
Unadjusted Trial Balance		
December 31, 2020		
Account Title	**Debit**	**Credit**
Cash	$ 6,200	
Accounts receivable	57,000	
Inventory	345,000	
Prepaid rent	28,000	
Equipment	108,000	
Accumulated amortization—equipment		$ 43,200
Accounts payable		43,200
Salary payable		0
Interest payable		0
Note payable, long-term		87,000
J. Marvin, capital		270,000
J. Marvin, withdrawals	153,000	
Sales revenue		835,400
Purchases	337,800	
Salary expense	118,600	
Rent expense	44,000	
Advertising expense	21,600	
Utilities expense	30,800	
Amortization expense—equipment	0	
Insurance expense	13,200	
Interest expense	2,600	
Miscellaneous expense	13,000	
Total	$1,278,800	$1,278,800

Additional data at December 31, 2020:

a. Rent expense for the year, $48,000.

b. The equipment has an estimated useful life of 10 years and is expected to have no value when it is retired from service.

c. Accrued salaries at December 31, $7,000.

d. Accrued interest expense at December 31, $2,600.

e. Inventory based on the inventory count on December 31, $351,200.

Required Complete Marvin's Fine Gems' worksheet for the year ended December 31, 2020. Key adjustments by letter. You do not need to complete the adjusted trial balance column as totals can be input directly into the financial statement columns. Marvin's Fine Gems uses the periodic inventory system.

MARVIN'S FINE GEMS
Worksheet
For the Year Ended December 31, 2020

ACCOUNT TITLE	UNADJUSTED TRIAL BALANCE DEBIT	UNADJUSTED TRIAL BALANCE CREDIT	ADJUSTMENTS DEBIT	ADJUSTMENTS CREDIT	INCOME STATEMENT DEBIT	INCOME STATEMENT CREDIT	BALANCE SHEET DEBIT	BALANCE SHEET CREDIT
Cash	$ 6,200							
Accounts receivable	57,000							
Inventory	345,000							
Prepaid rent	28,000							
Equipment	108,000							
Accum. amort.—equipment		$ 43,200						
Accounts payable		43,200						
Salary payable		0						
Interest payable		0						
Note payable, long-term		87,000						
J. Marvin, capital		270,000						
J. Marvin, withdrawals	153,000							
Sales revenue		835,400						
Purchases	337,800							
Salary expense	118,600							
Rent expense	44,000							
Advertising expense	21,600							
Utilities expense	30,800							
Amortization exp.—equipment	0							
Insurance expense	13,200							
Interest expense	2,600							
Miscellaneous expense	13,000							
	$1,278,800	$1,278,800						
Net income								

*P5–13A Ⓐ③

Refer to the data in P5–12A.

Required

1. Journalize the adjusting and closing entries.
2. Determine the December 31, 2020, balance of Capital for Marvin's Fine Gems.

Requirement 1

		Journal		
DATE	ACCOUNT TITLES AND EXPLANATIONS	POST REF.	DEBIT	CREDIT

Requirement 2 (December 31, 2020, balance of capital)

J. Marvin, Capital

Extra Journal Page				
DATE	ACCOUNT TITLES AND EXPLANATIONS	POST REF.	DEBIT	CREDIT

*P5–14A ⑤ Ⓐ④

Items from the accounts of Marchand Distributors at May 31, 2020, follow, listed in alphabetical order. Marchand Distributors uses the periodic inventory system. For simplicity, all operating expenses are summarized in the General Expenses and the Selling Expenses account.

Accounts Payable	$ 71,000		Inventory May 31, 2019	$ 151,800
Accounts Receivable	107,500		Note Payable, Long-Term	114,800
Accumulated Amortization—Equipment	96,900		Purchases	1,102,200
C. Marchand, Capital	167,800		Salaries Payable	7,200
C. Marchand, Withdrawals	66,900		Sales Discounts	26,500
Cash	19,900		Sales Returns and Allowances	45,900
Equipment	340,800		Sales Revenue	1,991,500
General Expenses	206,800		Selling Expenses	357,200
Interest Expense	9,200		Supplies	33,100
Interest Payable	2,800		Unearned Sales Revenue	15,200
Interest Revenue	600			

Required

1. Prepare the business's multi-step income statement for the year ended May 31, 2020. A physical count of inventory on May 31, 2020, valued it at $167,100.

2. Prepare Marchand Distributors' statement of owner's equity at May 31, 2020.

3. Prepare Marchand Distributors' classified balance sheet in report format at May 31, 2020.

4. Corry Marchand, owner of the company, strives to earn a gross margin of at least 50 percent and a net income of 20 percent (Net income percentage = Net income ÷ Net sales revenue). Did Marchand Distributors achieve these goals? Show your calculations. Round your answers to one decimal place.

Requirement 1

Requirement 2

Requirement 3

Requirement 4

Gross margin   =
   percentage

Net income   =
   percentage

6 ACCOUNTING FOR MERCHANDISE INVENTORY

LEARNING OBJECTIVES

1 Account for perpetual inventory under the specific-unit-cost, FIFO, and moving-weighted-average-cost methods.
2 Compare the effects of the FIFO and moving-weighted-average-cost methods.
3 Account for periodic inventory under the FIFO and weighted-average-cost methods.
4 Apply accounting concepts to inventory.
5 Estimate ending inventory by the gross margin method and the retail method.

SOME USEFUL TEXT INFORMATION (add your own notes too)

EXHIBIT 6–6 | Calculation of Cost of Goods Sold in a Periodic Inventory System

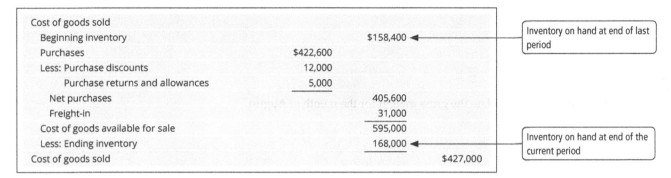

Cost of goods sold		
Beginning inventory		$158,400
Purchases	$422,600	
Less: Purchase discounts	12,000	
Purchase returns and allowances	5,000	
Net purchases		405,600
Freight-in		31,000
Cost of goods available for sale		595,000
Less: Ending inventory		168,000
Cost of goods sold		$427,000

Inventory on hand at end of last period

Inventory on hand at end of the current period

EXHIBIT 6–9 | Gross Margin Method of Estimating Inventory (amounts assumed)

Beginning inventory		$14,000
Net purchases		66,000
Cost of goods available for sale		80,000
Estimated cost of goods sold		
Sales revenue	$100,000	
Less: Estimated gross margin of 40%	40,000	
Estimated cost of goods sold (cost is 60% of sales revenue)		60,000
Estimated cost of ending inventory		$20,000
Equation solution: $14,000 + $66,000 − ($100,000 × 0.60) = $20,000		

EXHIBIT 6–10 | Retail Method of Estimating Inventory (amounts assumed)

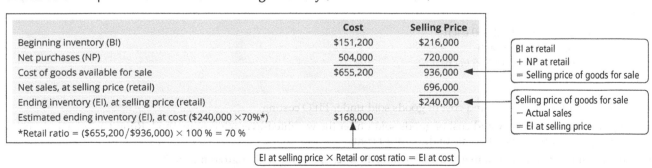

	Cost	Selling Price
Beginning inventory (BI)	$151,200	$216,000
Net purchases (NP)	504,000	720,000
Cost of goods available for sale	$655,200	936,000
Net sales, at selling price (retail)		696,000
Ending inventory (EI), at selling price (retail)		$240,000
Estimated ending inventory (EI), at cost ($240,000 ×70%*)	$168,000	
*Retail ratio = ($655,200/$936,000) × 100 % = 70 %		

BI at retail
+ NP at retail
= Selling price of goods for sale

Selling price of goods for sale
− Actual sales
= EI at selling price

EI at selling price × Retail or cost ratio = EI at cost

S6–1 ①

Garda's Equipment has the following items in its inventory on August 1:

Serial Number	Cost
6X6A1	$ 9,100
6Y6M5	9,300
6B6D8	8,700
6R7R5	10,950

The company uses the specific-unit-cost method for costing inventory. During August, it sold units 6X6A1 and 6B6B8 for $15,000 each and purchased unit 6A7M6 for $11,200. What is the value of the ending inventory at August 31?

_____

_____

_____

_____

_____

S6–2 ①

Refer to the information in S6–1. Calculate the gross margin for the month of August.

_____

_____

_____

_____

_____

S6–9 ③

Kim's Shirt and Tie Shop uses a periodic inventory system. Kim's completed the following inventory transactions during April, its first month of operations:

Apr. 1 Purchased 10 shirts at $50 each
      7 Sold 6 shirts for $80 each
     13 Purchased 6 shirts for $55 each
     21 Sold 3 shirts for $85 each

a. Compute Kim's ending inventory and cost of goods sold under FIFO costing.

b. Then compute ending inventory and cost of goods sold under the weighted-average-cost method. Round average unit cost to three decimal places, but round all totals to the nearest cent.

c. Compute gross margin under both methods. Which method results in the higher gross margin?

	a. FIFO	b. Weighted Average

c.

_____

_____

_____

S6–11 ④

Determine the value of the inventory to be reported on the balance sheet by applying lower-of-cost-and-net-realizable-value rule to the following data:

Item	Quantity	Cost Price/Unit	Market Price/Unit	Selling Costs
001	5	$29	$30	$100
002	8	$40	$35	$ 50

S6–12 ④

Trump Luggage Sales uses a periodic inventory system. The inventory data for the year ended December 31, 2019, follow:

Sales revenue		$150,000
Cost of goods sold		
Beginning inventory	22,000	
Net purchases	80,000	
Cost of goods available for sale	102,000	
Less: Ending inventory	24,000	
Cost of goods sold	78,000	
Gross margin		$72,000

Assume that the ending inventory was accidentally overstated by $4,000. What are the correct amounts of cost of goods sold and gross margin after correcting this error?

_____

_____

_____

_____

_____

_____

_____

_____

S6–14 ⑤

Magic Carpets began the year with inventory of $1,400,000. Inventory purchases for the year totalled $3,200,000. Sales revenue for the year was $7,000,000 and the gross margin was 45 percent. How much is Magic Carpets's estimated cost of ending inventory? Use the gross margin method.

E6–2 ①

Elmo's Music carries a large inventory of guitars and other musical instruments. The store uses the FIFO method and a perpetual inventory system. Company records indicate the following for a particular line of guitars that sell for $1,600 each:

Date		Item	Quantity	Unit Cost
May	1	Balance	5	$900
	6	Sale	3	
	8	Purchase	10	840
	17	Sale	4	
	30	Purchase	5	840

Required   Prepare a perpetual inventory record for the guitars. Then determine the amounts Elmo's Music should report for ending inventory and cost of goods sold under the FIFO method.

Perpetual Inventory Record

ITEM:

		PURCHASES			COST OF GOODS SOLD			INVENTORY ON HAND	
DATE	QTY.	UNIT COST	TOTAL COST	QTY.	UNIT COST	TOTAL COST	QTY.	UNIT COST	TOTAL COST

Calculations:

E6-3 ①

After preparing the FIFO perpetual inventory record in E6-2, journalize Elmo's Music's May 8 purchase of inventory on account and the cash sale on May 17.

Journal				
DATE	ACCOUNT TITLES AND EXPLANATIONS	POST REF.	DEBIT	CREDIT

E6–4 ①

Refer to the Elmo's Music inventory data in E6–2, except assume that the store uses the moving-weighted-average-cost method. Prepare Elmo's Music Store's perpetual inventory record for the guitars on the moving-weighted-average-cost basis. Round average cost per unit to the nearest cent and all other amounts to the nearest dollar.

Perpetual Inventory Record

ITEM:

DATE	QTY.	UNIT COST	TOTAL COST	QTY.	UNIT COST	TOTAL COST	QTY.	UNIT COST	TOTAL COST
		PURCHASES			COST OF GOODS SOLD			INVENTORY ON HAND	

Calculations:

E6–7 ②

Use your results from E6-2, E6-3, and E6–4 to calculate the gross margin for Elmo's Music under both the FIFO and the moving-weighted-average-cost methods. Explain why the gross margin is higher under the moving-weighted-average-cost method.

	FIFO	Moving-Weighted-Average

E6-11 ③

Kelso Electrical's inventory records for industrial switches indicate the following at November 30, 2020:

Nov.	1	Beginning inventory	14 units at $160
	8	Purchase	4 units at $170
	15	Purchase	11 units at $180
	26	Purchase	5 units at $190

The physical count of inventory at November 30, 2020, indicates that six units remain in ending inventory and the company owns them.

Required Compute ending inventory and cost of goods sold using each of the following methods, assuming a periodic inventory system is used:

1. Specific-unit cost, assuming three $170 units and three $180 units are on hand on November 30, 2020
2. Weighted-average cost
3. First-in, first-out (FIFO)

Requirements 1 – 3

	ENDING INVENTORY	COST OF GOODS SOLD

1. SPECIFIC-UNIT COST:

2. WEIGHTED-AVERAGE COST:

3. FIFO COST:

E6–14 ③ ④

Before the following financial statement was released, it was discovered that the current net realizable value of ending inventory was $96,000.
1. Journalize the entry to apply the lower-of-cost-and-net-realizable-value rule to the inventory on August 31, 2020. No explanation is required.
2. Prepare a revised income statement to apply the lower-of-cost-and-net-realizable-value rule to Wire Solutions Company's inventory.
3. What is the inventory balance that would be reported on the Wire Solutions Company's balance sheet. How would it be reported?

WIRE SOLUTIONS COMPANY		
Income Statement (partial)		
For the Month Ended August 31, 2020		
Sales revenue		$320,000
Cost of goods sold		
Beginning inventory	$ 82,000	
Net purchases	243,700	
Cost of goods available for sale	325,700	
Less: Ending inventory	105,700	
Cost of goods sold		220,000
Gross margin		$100,000

Requirement 1

Journal					
DATE		ACCOUNT TITLES AND EXPLANATIONS	POST REF.	DEBIT	CREDIT

Requirement 2

Requirement 3

E6-21 ② Serial Exercise

The Serial Exercise involves a company that will be revisited throughout relevant chapters in Volume 1 and Volume 2. You can complete the Serial Exercises using MyLab Accounting.

This exercise continues recordkeeping for the Canyon Canoe Company. You do not have to have completed any previous questions to complete this exercise.

At the beginning of January 2021, Canyon Canoe Company decided to carry and sell T-shirts with its logo printed on them. Canyon Canoe Company uses the perpetual inventory system to account for the inventory. During February 2021, Canyon Canoe Company completed the following merchandising transactions:

Feb.	2	Sold 60 T-shirts at $10 each.
	5	Purchased 50 T-shirts at $6 each.
	7	Sold 45 T-shirts for $10 each.
	8	Sold 20 T-shirts for $10 each.
	10	Canyon Canoe Company realized the inventory was running low, so it placed a rush order and purchased 20 T-shirts. The premium cost for these shirts was $7 each.
	12	Placed a second rush order and purchased 40 T-shirts at $7 each.
	13	Sold 20 T-shirts for $10 each.
	15	Purchased 50 T-shirts at $6 each.
	20	In order to avoid future rush orders, purchased 150 T-shirts. Due to the volume of the order, Canyon Canoe Company was able to negotiate a cost of $5 each.
	21	Sold 40 T-shirts for $10 each.
	22	Sold 35 T-shirts for $10 each.
	24	Sold 20 T-shirts for $10 each.
	25	Sold 45 T-shirts for $10 each.
	27	Sold 40 T-shirts for $10 each.

Required

1. Assume Canyon Canoe Company began February with 94 T-shirts in inventory that cost $5 each. Prepare the perpetual inventory records for February using the FIFO inventory costing method.

2. Provide a summary for the month, in both units and dollars, of the change in inventory in the following format:

	Number of T-shirts	Dollar Amount
Beginning Balance		
Add: Purchases		
Less: Cost of Goods Sold		
Ending Balance		

Students, complete requirement 2 here after you record the requirement 1 information on the next page.

Requirement 1

Perpetual Inventory Record

ITEM:

DATE	PURCHASES			COST OF GOODS SOLD			INVENTORY ON HAND		
	QTY.	UNIT COST	TOTAL COST	QTY.	UNIT COST	TOTAL COST	QTY.	UNIT COST	TOTAL COST

P6–2A ①

PEI Distributors purchases inventory in crates of merchandise. Assume the company began July with an inventory of 30 units that cost $300 each. During the month, the company engaged in the following business transactions:

Jul. 10   Purchased 30 units on account at $320.
  15   Sold 40 units on account at $700.
  22   Purchased 70 units on account at $350.
  29   Sold 75 units on account at $800.
  31   Reported monthly operating expenses of $30,000. The company paid
        one-third with cash and the rest was recorded on account.
  31   Paid $12,000 of the Accounts Payable balance

Assume PEI Distributors uses the FIFO cost method for valuing inventories. The company uses a perpetual inventory system.

Required

1. Prepare a perpetual inventory record, at FIFO cost, for this merchandise.
2. Make journal entries to record the company's transactions. No explanations are necessary.

Requirement 1

Perpetual Inventory Record

ITEM:

		PURCHASES			COST OF GOODS SOLD			INVENTORY ON HAND	
DATE	QTY.	UNIT COST	TOTAL COST	QTY.	UNIT COST	TOTAL COST	QTY.	UNIT COST	TOTAL COST

Requirement 2

	Journal				
DATE		ACCOUNT TITLES AND EXPLANATIONS	POST REF.	DEBIT	CREDIT

P6–4A ②

Refer to the PEI Distributors situation in P6–2A. Keep all the data unchanged, except assume that the company uses the moving-weighted-average-cost method.

Required

1. Prepare a perpetual inventory record using the moving-weighted-average cost. Round the average unit cost to the nearest cent and all other amounts to the nearest dollar.
2. Prepare a multi-step income statement for PEI Distributors for the month of July 2020 to calculate operating income.

Requirement 1

		**Perpetual Inventory Record**
ITEM:										
		PURCHASES			COST OF GOODS SOLD			INVENTORY ON HAND		
DATE	QTY.	UNIT COST	TOTAL COST	QTY.	UNIT COST	TOTAL COST	QTY.	UNIT COST	TOTAL COST	

Requirement 2

P6–6A ① ②

Gamsu's Office Depot sells office furniture. The company's fiscal year ends on March 31, 2020. On January 1, 2020, inventory consisted of 20 office dividers that cost $1,800 each. During the quarter, Gamsu's purchased inventory on account as follows:

	Units	Unit Cost	Total
January	60	$1,850	$111,000
February	40	1,900	76,000
March	30	1,950	58,500

Sales for each month in the quarter were as follows:

	Units	Unit Selling Price	Total
January	50	$3,600	$180,000
February	20	3,700	74,000
March	34	3,800	129,200

Operating expenses in the quarter were $110,000.

Assume that the company uses a perpetual inventory system and that purchases of inventory occur on the first day of each month.

Required

1. Determine the cost of the divider ending inventory at March 31, 2020, under (a) moving-weighted-average costing and (b) FIFO costing. Round the average unit cost to the nearest cent and all other amounts to the nearest dollar.
2. Prepare a multi-step income statement for the quarter ended March 31, 2020, under each method described in Requirement 1.

Requirement 1

a.

Perpetual Inventory Record

ITEM:										
		PURCHASES			COST OF GOODS SOLD			INVENTORY ON HAND		
DATE	QTY.	UNIT COST	TOTAL COST	QTY.	UNIT COST	TOTAL COST	QTY.	UNIT COST	TOTAL COST	

b.

		PURCHASES			COST OF GOODS SOLD			INVENTORY ON HAND	
DATE	QTY.	UNIT COST	TOTAL COST	QTY.	UNIT COST	TOTAL COST	QTY.	UNIT COST	TOTAL COST

Perpetual Inventory Record

ITEM:

Requirement 2

	MOVING-WEIGHTED-AVERAGE	FIFO

P6-8A ③

Pongphop Noodles began April with 73 units of inventory that cost $50 each. During the month, Pongphop made the following purchases:

Apr.	4	113 units at $48
	12	81 units at $49
	19	167 units at $52
	25	34 units at $56

The company uses a periodic inventory system, and the physical count at April 30 shows 51 units of inventory on hand.

Required

1. Determine the ending inventory and cost of goods sold amounts for the April financial statements under (a) weighted-average cost and (b) FIFO cost. Round average cost per unit to the nearest cent and all other amounts to the nearest dollar.

2. Sales revenue for April totalled $40,000. Compute Pongphop's gross margin for April under each method.

3. Which method will result in higher net income for Pongphop? Why?

Requirement 1

(a) WEIGHTED-AVERAGE COST

(b) FIFO COST

Requirement 2

	WEIGHTED-AVERAGE	FIFO

Requirement 3

P6–14A ① ⑤

Danilov Computers uses a perpetual inventory system for the purchase and sale of their SSD inventory and had the following information available on November 30, 2020:

		Purchases and Sales	Number of Units
Nov.	1	Balance of inventory at $40 per unit	3,900
	7	Purchased at $56 per unit	6,000
	8	Sold for $76 each	4,500
	12	Purchased at $52 per unit	7,500
	16	Sold for $84 each	9,000
	21	Purchased at $52 per unit	4,500
	25	Purchased at $48 per unit	10,500
	29	Sold for $84 each	13,500

Required

1. Calculate the cost of goods sold and the cost of the ending inventory for November under each of the following inventory costing methods: (a) moving-weighted-average cost and (b) FIFO cost.

2. Prepare the journal entries required to record the transactions using the perpetual inventory system with FIFO costing.

3. An internal audit has discovered that a new employee—an accounting clerk—had been stealing merchandise and covering up the shortage by changing the inventory records. The external auditors examined the accounting records prior to the employment of the individual and noted that the company has an average gross margin rate of 37 percent. Use the gross margin method to estimate the cost of the inventory shortage (under the FIFO costing method). (Note: The physical count matched the estimate.) Explain the difference between the three inventory values—the accounting records, physical count, and estimates—and their importance in valuing inventory.

Requirement 1

Perpetual Inventory Record

ITEM:

DATE	QTY.	PURCHASES UNIT COST	TOTAL COST	QTY.	COST OF GOODS SOLD UNIT COST	TOTAL COST	QTY.	INVENTORY ON HAND UNIT COST	TOTAL COST

Perpetual Inventory Record

ITEM:

DATE	QTY.	PURCHASES UNIT COST	TOTAL COST	QTY.	COST OF GOODS SOLD UNIT COST	TOTAL COST	QTY.	INVENTORY ON HAND UNIT COST	TOTAL COST

Requirement 2

Journal

DATE	ACCOUNT TITLES AND EXPLANATIONS	POST REF.	DEBIT	CREDIT

Requirement 3

Extra Journal Page

DATE		ACCOUNT TITLES AND EXPLANATIONS	POST REF.	DEBIT	CREDIT

7 ACCOUNTING INFORMATION SYSTEMS

LEARNING OBJECTIVES

1 Describe an effective accounting information system.
2 Explain the elements of computerized and manual accounting systems.
3 Journalize and post transactions using the sales journal, the cash receipts journal, and the accounts receivable subsidiary ledger.
4 Journalize and post transactions using the purchases journal, the cash payments journal, and the accounts payable subsidiary ledger.
5 Journalize and post entries not recorded in a special journal.

*A1 Use special journals to record and post transactions with sales taxes. (found on MyLab Accounting)

SOME USEFUL TEXT INFORMATION (add your own notes too)

EXHIBIT 7–5 | An Accounting System with Special Journals for a Merchandising Business

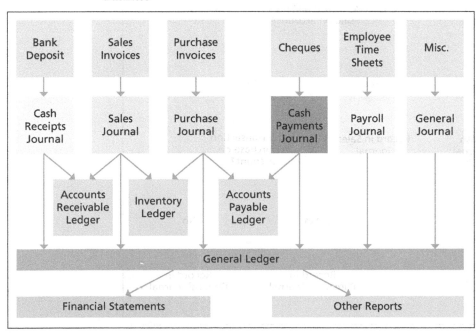

EXHIBIT 7–11 | A Method of Choosing the Special Journal to Use for a Transaction

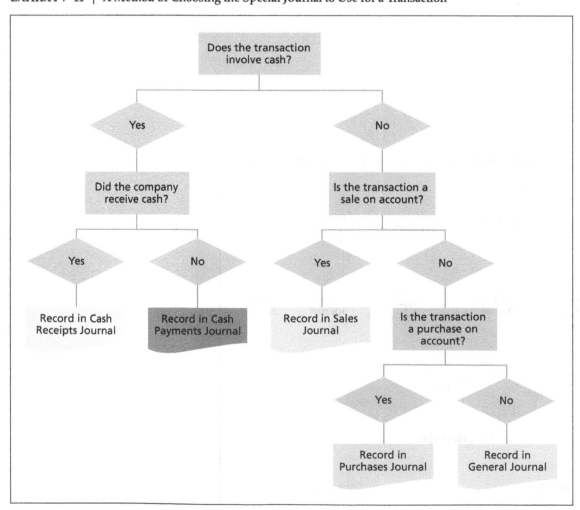

S7–3 ① ②

Complete the crossword puzzle.

Across:

2. Electronic linkage that allows different computers to share the same information
3. Main computer in a networked system
7. Cost–_____ relationship must be favourable

Down:

1. Managers need _____ over operations to authorize transactions and safeguard assets
3. Programs that drive a computer
4. Electronic computer equipment
5. A _____ ible information system accommodates changes as the organization evolves
6. The opposite of debits

S7–6 ②

From the list below, identify the headings and the account names of LP Gas Co. Assign an account number to each account.

Assets	_____
Current Assets	_____
Inventory	_____
Accounts Payable	_____
LP, Capital	_____
LP, Withdrawals	_____
Revenues	_____
Selling Expenses	_____

Numbers from which to choose:

151	301
191	311
201	411
281	531

S7-15 ③ ④ ⑤

Use the following abbreviations to indicate the journal in which you would record transactions a through o:

G = General journal   P = Purchases journal

S = Sales journal   CP = Cash payments journal

CR = Cash receipts journal

Transactions:

a. _____ Cash sale of inventory

b. _____ Payment of rent

c. _____ Amortization of computer equipment

d. _____ Purchases of inventory on account

e. _____ Collection of accounts receivable

f. _____ Expiration of prepaid insurance

g. _____ Sale on account

h. _____ Payment on account

i. _____ Cash purchase of inventory

j. _____ Collection of dividend revenue earned on an investment

k. _____ Prepayment of insurance

l. _____ Borrowing money on a long-term note payable

m. _____ Purchase of equipment on account

n. _____ Cost of goods sold along with a credit sale

o. _____ Return of merchandise

E7–2

It is very important to set up a properly numbered chart of accounts, especially in a computerized accounting system. Use account numbers 101 through 106, 201, 221, 301, 321, 401, 501, and 521 to correspond to the following selected accounts from the general ledger of Kelowna Music Festival. List the accounts and their account numbers in proper order, starting with the most liquid current asset.

_____ M. Wyant, Capital

_____ Accounts Receivable

_____ Cash

_____ Accounts Payable

_____ Music Equipment

_____ Supplies

_____ Accumulated Amortization—Music Equipment

_____ Amortization Expense—Music Equipment

_____ Cost of Goods Sold

_____ Note Payable, Long-Term

_____ M. Wyant, Withdrawals

_____ Inventory

_____ Sales Revenue

E7-6 ③

During February, Sanier Animation had the following transactions:

Feb. 1 Sold merchandise inventory on account to Theatre Co., $1,025. Cost of goods, $780. Invoice no. 401.

6 Sold merchandise inventory for cash, $860 (cost, $640).

12 Collected interest revenue of $80.

15 Received cash from Theatre Co. in full settlement of its account receivable. There was no discount.

20 Sold merchandise inventory on account to Delgado Co., issuing invoice no. 402 for $440 (cost, $330).

22 Sold merchandise inventory for cash, $560 (cost, $420).

26 Sold office supplies to an employee for cash of $80.

28 Received $431 from Delgado Co. in full settlement of its account receivable. Delgado earned a discount by paying early. Terms are 2/10, n/15.

Required

1. Journalize the transactions that should be recorded in Page 9 of the sales journal. (Round the sales discount to a whole dollar.) Assume the company uses a perpetual inventory system.
2. Total each column of the sales journal.

Requirements 1 & 2

Sales Journal					PAGE
DATE	INVOICE NO.	ACCOUNT DEBITED	POST REF.	ACCOUNT RECEIVABLE DR. SALES REVENUE CR.	COST OF GOODS SOLD DR. INVENTORY CR.

E7–7 ③

Refer to the information in E7–6.

Required

1. Journalize the transactions that should be recorded in the cash receipts journal.
2. Total each column of the cash receipts journal.

Cash Receipts Journal

PAGE

| DATE | DEBITS | | CREDITS | | OTHER ACCOUNTS | | | |
	CASH	SALES DISCOUNTS	ACCOUNTS RECEIVABLE	SALES REVENUE	ACCOUNT TITLE	POST REF.	AMOUNT	COST OF GOODS SOLD DR. INVENTORY CR.

E7-13 ④

Bright's Patio Shop sells garden and patio furniture. Record the following transactions in the appropriate special journals. Total each journal at May 31.

May 1   Sold $2,600 of patio furniture to Jen Williams, terms n/30, invoice 310 (cost, $1,700).

2   Purchased inventory on credit terms of 1/10, n/60 from Sisco Corp., $8,000. Invoice date is May 2.

5   Sold inventory for cash, $400 (cost, $220).

10   Purchased $600 of patio lanterns from an artisan. Issued cheque no. 401.

15   Sold $5,000 of outdoor seating to Pat's Restaurant, terms n/30, invoice 311 (cost, $3,400).

22   Received payment from Jen Williams (May 1).

26   Received payment from Pat's Restaurant (May 15).

29   Paid Sisco Corp. for the purchase made on May 2, cheque no. 402.

	Sales Journal				
DATE	ACCOUNT DEBITED		POST REF.	ACCOUNT RECEIVABLE DR. SALES REVENUE CR.	COST OF GOODS SOLD DR. INVENTORY CR.

Cash Receipt Journal

PAGE

DATE	DEBITS	CREDITS					COST OF GOODS SOLD DR. INVENTORY CR.
	CASH	ACCOUNTS RECEIVABLE	SALES REVENUE	SERVICE REVENUE	OTHER ACCOUNTS		
					ACCOUNT TITLE	POST REF.	AMOUNT	

Purchases Journal

PAGE

DATE	ACCOUNT CREDITED	INV. DATE	TERMS	POST REF.	CREDITS	DEBITS		
					ACCOUNTS PAYABLE	INVENTORY	OTHER ACCOUNTS	
							ACCOUNT TITLE	POST REF.	AMOUNT

Cash Payments Journal

PAGE

DATE	CHQ. NO.	ACCOUNT DEBITED	POST REF.	CREDITS		DEBITS		
				OTHER ACCOUNTS	ACCOUNTS PAYABLE	SALARY PAYABLE	INVENTORY	CASH

E7–14 ④ ⑤

During April, Xitang Company completed the following credit purchase transactions:

Apr. 5 Purchased supplies, $400, from Central Co.

11 Purchased inventory, $1,200, from McDonald Ltd. Xitang Company uses a perpetual inventory system.

14 Issued cheque to pay Central Co.

19 Purchased equipment, $4,300, from Baker Corp.

20 Issued cheque to pay Baker Corp.

22 Purchased inventory, $2,210, from Khalil Inc.

Required Record these transactions first in the general journal—with explanations—and then in the purchases journal. Omit credit terms, posting references, and invoice dates. After setting up the purchases journal form, which procedure for recording transactions is quicker? Why?

General Journal

DATE	ACCOUNT TITLES AND EXPLANATIONS	POST REF.	DEBIT	CREDIT

Purchases Journal

DATE	ACCOUNT CREDITED	INV. DATE	TERMS	POST REF.	CREDITS ACCOUNTS PAYABLE	INVENTORY	SUPPLIES	DEBITS OTHER ACCOUNTS ACCOUNT TITLE	POST REF.	AMOUNT

E7-15 ③⑤

M and N Sporting Goods reported these selected transactions for the month of July:

Jul. 9 Issued invoice no. 159 for a sale on account to Evans Company, $4,600, terms 1/10, n/30. The cost of the merchandise was $2,700.

10 Issued invoice no. 160 for a sale on account to Sails and Boats, $5,700, terms 2/15, n/45. The cost of the merchandise was $2,450.

12 Sold $3,000 of merchandise to Bruce Services for cash. The cost of the merchandise was $1,250.

16 Owner invested $3,400 into the business.

18 Collected $580 from Lucille Adams on account.

20 Issued a credit memo to Sails and Boats for $2,800 for merchandise returned. The cost of the returned merchandise was $1,200.

Required Record the above transactions in either the sales journal, the cash receipts journal, or the general journal. M and N Sporting Goods uses a perpetual inventory system.

Sales Journal

DATE		ACCOUNT DEBITED	POST REF.	ACCOUNT RECEIVABLE DR. SALES REVENUE CR.	COST OF GOODS SOLD DR. INVENTORY CR.

General Journal

DATE		ACCOUNT TITLES AND EXPLANATIONS	POST REF.	DEBIT	CREDIT

Cash Receipts Journal

PAGE

| DATE | DEBITS | | CREDITS | | OTHER ACCOUNTS | | | |
	CASH	SALES DISCOUNTS	ACCOUNTS RECEIVABLE	SALES REVENUE	ACCOUNT TITLE	POST REF.	AMOUNT	COST OF GOODS SOLD DR. INVENTORY CR.

E7–16 ③ ④ ⑤   Serial Exercise

The Serial Exercise involves a company that will be revisited throughout relevant chapters in Volume 1 and Volume 2. You can complete the Serial Exercises using MyLab Accounting.

This exercise continues recordkeeping for the Canyon Canoe Company. You do not have to have completed any previous questions to complete this exercise.

At the beginning of the new year, Canyon Canoe Company decided to carry and sell T-shirts with its logo printed on them. Canyon Canoe Company uses the perpetual inventory system to account for the inventory. During January 2021, Canyon Canoe Company completed the following merchandising transactions:

Jan. 1   Purchased 10 T-shirts at $4 each and paid cash.

2   Sold 6 T-shirts for $10 each, total cost of $24. Received cash.

3   Purchased 50 T-shirts on account at $5 each. Terms 2/10, n/30.

7   Paid the supplier for the T-shirts purchased on January 3, less discount.

8   Realized 4 T-shirts from the January 1 order were printed wrong and returned them for a cash refund.

10   Sold 40 T-shirts on account for $10 each, total cost of $200. Terms 3/15, n/45.

12   Received payment for the T-shirts sold on account on January 10, less discount.

14   Purchased 100 T-shirts on account at $4 each. Terms 4/15, n/30.

18   Canyon Company called the supplier from the January 14 purchase and told them that some of the T-shirts were the wrong colour. The supplier offered a $50 purchase allowance.

20   Paid the supplier for the T-shirts purchased on January 14, less the allowance and discount.

21   Sold 60 T-shirts on account for $10 each, total cost of $220. Terms 2/20, n/30.

23   Received a payment on account for the T-shirts sold on January 21, less discount.

25   Purchased 320 T-shirts on account at $5 each. Terms 2/10, n/30, FOB shipping point.

27   Paid freight associated with the January 25 purchase, $48.

29   Paid for the January 25 purchase, less discount.

30   Sold 275 T-shirts on account for $10 each, total cost of $1,300. Terms 2/10, n/30.

31   Received payment for the T-shirts sold on January 30

Required

1. Enter the transactions in a sales journal (Page 2, omit the invoice number column), a cash receipts journal (Page 5), a purchases journal (Page 7, omit the supplier name and invoice date column), a cash payments journal (Page 6, omit the cheque number and payee), and a general journal (Page 4), as appropriate.

2. Total each column of the special journals. Show that total debits equal total credits in each special journal.

Sales Journal

PAGE

DATE		CUSTOMER ACCOUNT DEBITED	POST REF.	ACCOUNTS RECEIVABLE DR. SALES REVENUE CR.	COST OF GOODS SOLD DR. INVENTORY CR.

General Journal

PAGE

DATE		ACCOUNTS AND EXPLANATION	POST REF.	DEBIT	CREDIT

Cash Receipts Journal

PAGE

DATE	DEBITS		CREDITS		OTHER ACCOUNTS			
	CASH	SALES DISCOUNTS	ACCOUNTS RECEIVABLE	SALES REVENUE	ACCOUNT TITLE	POST REF.	AMOUNT	COST OF GOODS SOLD DR. INVENTORY CR.

Purchases Journal

PAGE

DATE	SUPPLIER ACCOUNT CREDITED	INV. DATE	TERMS	POST REF.	CREDITS ACCOUNTS PAYABLE	DEBITS INVENTORY	SUPPLIES	OTHER ACCOUNTS ACCOUNT TITLE	POST REF.	AMOUNT

Cash Payments Journal

PAGE

DATE	CHQ. NO.	PAYEE	ACCOUNT DEBITED	POST REF.	DEBIT OTHER ACCOUNTS	ACCOUNTS PAYABLE	CREDIT INVENTORY	CASH

P7-4A ③ ④ ⑤

The Nova Scotia Beekeepers Supply Company, which uses the perpetual inventory system and makes all credit sales on terms of 2/10, n/30, completed the following transactions during July. The business records all sales returns and all purchase returns in the general journal.

Jul. 2   Issued invoice no. 913 for sale on account to White Harbour Restaurant, $12,300. The cost of this inventory was $5,400.

3   Purchased inventory on credit terms of 3/10, n/60 from The Country Store, $7,401. The invoice was dated July 3.

5   Sold inventory for cash, $3,231 (cost, $1,440).

5   Issued cheque no. 532 to purchase beekeeping equipment for cash, $6,555.

8   Collected interest revenue of $3,325.

9   Issued invoice no. 914 for sale on account to Bell Ltd., $16,650 (cost, $6,930).

10   Purchased inventory for cash, $3,429, issuing cheque no. 533.

12   Received cash from White Harbour Restaurant in full settlement of its account receivable from the sale on July 2.

13   Issued cheque no. 534 to pay The Country Store the net amount owed from July 3.

13   Purchased supplies on account from Manley Inc., $4,323. Terms were net end of month. The invoice was dated July 12.

15   Sold inventory on account to O. Brown, issuing invoice no. 915 for $1,995 (cost, $720).

17   Issued credit memo to O. Brown for $1,995 for merchandise sent in error and returned by Brown. Also accounted for receipt of the inventory.

18   Issued invoice no. 916 for credit sale to White Harbour Restaurant, $1,071 (cost, $381).

19   Received $16,317 from Bell Ltd. in full settlement of its account receivable from July 9.

20   Purchased inventory on credit terms of net 30 from Burgess Distributing Ltd., $6,141. The invoice was dated July 20.

22   Purchased furniture on credit terms of 3/10, n/60 from The Country Store, $1,935. The invoice was dated July 22.

22   Issued cheque no. 535 to pay for insurance coverage, debiting Prepaid Insurance for $3,000.

24   Sold supplies to an employee for cash of $162, which was the cost of the supplies.

25   Issued cheque no. 536 to pay utilities, $3,359

28   Purchased inventory on credit terms of 2/10, n/30 from Manley Inc., $4,025. The invoice was dated July 28.

29   Returned damaged inventory to Manley Inc., issuing a debit memo for $2,025.

29   Sold goods on account to Bell Ltd., issuing invoice no. 917 for $1,488 (cost, $660).

30   Issued cheque no. 537 to pay Manley Inc. $1,323.

31   Received cash in full on account from White Harbour Restaurant.

31   Issued cheque no. 538 to pay monthly salaries of $7,041.

Required   Use the following abbreviations to indicate the journal in which you would record each of the July transactions. Key each transaction by date. Also indicate whether the transaction would be recorded in the accounts receivable subsidiary ledger or the accounts payable subsidiary ledger.

G = General journal   P = Purchases journal

S = Sales journal   CP = Cash payments journal

CR = Cash receipts journal

Date	Journal	Subsidiary Ledger
July 2	_____	_____
3	_____	_____
5	_____	_____
5	_____	_____
8	_____	_____
9	_____	_____
10	_____	_____
12	_____	_____
13	_____	_____
13	_____	_____
15	_____	_____
17	_____	_____
18	_____	_____
19	_____	_____
20	_____	_____
22	_____	_____
22	_____	_____
24	_____	_____
25	_____	_____
28	_____	_____
29	_____	_____
29	_____	_____
30	_____	_____
31	_____	_____
31	_____	_____

P7–5A ③ ⑤

The general ledger of Yilin Groceries includes the following selected accounts, along with their account numbers:

Cash..	11	Land	18
Accounts Receivable..	12	Sales Revenue	41
Inventory	13	Sales Discounts	42
Notes Receivable	15	Sales Returns and Allowances	43
Supplies	16	Cost of Goods Sold..	51

All credit sales are on the company's standard terms of 2/10, n/30. Transactions in July that affected sales and cash receipts were as follows:

Jul.	2	Sold inventory on credit to Fortin Inc., $2,800. Yilin's cost of these goods was $1,600.
	4	As a favour to a competitor, sold supplies at cost, $3,400, receiving cash.
	7	Cash sales of merchandise for the week totalled $7,560 (cost, $6,560).
	9	Sold merchandise on account to A. L. Price, $29,280 (cost, $20,440).
	10	Sold land that cost $50,000 for cash of $50,000.
	11	Sold goods on account to Sloan Forge Ltd., $20,416 (cost, $14,080).
	12	Received cash from Fortin Inc. in full settlement of its account receivable from July 2.
	14	Cash sales of merchandise for the week were $8,424 (cost, $6,120).
	15	Sold inventory on credit to the partnership of Wilkie & Blinn, $14,600 (cost, $9,040).
	18	Received inventory sold on July 9 to A. L. Price for $2,400. The goods shipped were the wrong size. These goods cost $1,760.
	20	Sold merchandise on account to Sloan Forge Ltd., $2,516 (cost, $1,800).
	21	Cash sales of merchandise for the week were $3,960 (cost, $2,760).
	22	Received $8,000 cash from A. L. Price in partial settlement of his account receivable.
	25	Received cash from Wilkie & Blinn for its account receivable from July 15.
	25	Sold goods on account to Olsen Inc., $6,080 (cost, $4,200).
	27	Collected $10,500 on a note receivable.
	28	Cash sales of merchandise for the week were $15,096 (cost, $9,840).
	29	Sold inventory on account to R. O. Bankston Inc., $968 (cost, $680).
	30	Received goods sold on July 25 to Olsen Inc. for $160. The wrong items were shipped. The cost of the goods was $100.
	31	Received $18,880 cash on account from A. L. Price.

Required

1. Use the appropriate journal to record the above transactions: a sales journal (omit the Invoice No. column), a cash receipts journal, or a general journal. Yilin Groceries records sales returns and allowances in the general journal.
2. Total each column of the sales journal and the cash receipts journal. Show that total debits equal total credits.
3. Show how postings would be made from the journals by writing the account numbers and check marks in the appropriate places in the journals.

Please note that optional ledgers are included so that you can practice posting.

Requirements 1 – 3

Sales Journal

DATE		ACCOUNTS DEBITED	POST REF.	ACCOUNTS RECEIVABLE DR. SALES REVENUE CR.	COST OF GOODS SOLD DR. INVENTORY CR.

General Journal

DATE		ACCOUNT TITLES AND EXPLANATIONS	POST REF.	DEBIT	CREDIT

Requirements 1 – 3 (Continued)

Cash Receipts Journal

PAGE _____

DATE	DEBITS			CREDITS					
	CASH	SALES DISCOUNTS	ACCOUNTS RECEIVABLE	SALES REVENUE	OTHER ACCOUNTS			COST OF GOODS SOLD DR. INVENTORY CR.
					ACCOUNT TITLE	POST REF.	AMOUNT	

Optional Ledgers
Accounts Receivable Subsidiary Ledger

ACCOUNT					
DATE	ITEM	JRNL. REF.	DEBIT	CREDIT	BALANCE

ACCOUNT					
DATE	ITEM	JRNL. REF.	DEBIT	CREDIT	BALANCE

ACCOUNT					
DATE	ITEM	JRNL. REF.	DEBIT	CREDIT	BALANCE

ACCOUNT					
DATE	ITEM	JRNL. REF.	DEBIT	CREDIT	BALANCE

ACCOUNT					
DATE	ITEM	JRNL. REF.	DEBIT	CREDIT	BALANCE

ACCOUNT					
DATE	ITEM	JRNL. REF.	DEBIT	CREDIT	BALANCE

General Ledger (selected accounts)

ACCOUNT		CASH				ACCOUNT NO. 11
DATE		ITEM	JRNL. REF.	DEBIT	CREDIT	BALANCE
Jun.	30	Assumed bal. fwd.				73,880

ACCOUNT		ACCOUNTS RECEIVABLE				ACCOUNT NO. 12
DATE		ITEM	JRNL. REF.	DEBIT	CREDIT	BALANCE
Jun.	30	Assumed bal. fwd.				73,441

ACCOUNT	INVENTORY					ACCOUNT NO. 13
DATE		ITEM	JRNL. REF.	DEBIT	CREDIT	BALANCE
Jun.	30	Assumed bal. fwd.				392,881

ACCOUNT	NOTES RECEIVABLE					ACCOUNT NO. 15
DATE		ITEM	JRNL. REF.	DEBIT	CREDIT	BALANCE
Jun.	30	Assumed bal. fwd.				10,500

ACCOUNT	SUPPLIES					ACCOUNT NO. 16
DATE		ITEM	JRNL. REF.	DEBIT	CREDIT	BALANCE
Jun.	30	Assumed bal. fwd.				7,700

ACCOUNT	LAND					ACCOUNT NO. 18
DATE		ITEM	JRNL. REF.	DEBIT	CREDIT	BALANCE
Jun.	30	Assumed bal. fwd.				50,000

ACCOUNT	SALES REVENUE				ACCOUNT NO. 41	
DATE		ITEM	JRNL. REF.	DEBIT	CREDIT	BALANCE

ACCOUNT	SALES DISCOUNTS				ACCOUNT NO. 42	
DATE		ITEM	JRNL. REF.	DEBIT	CREDIT	BALANCE

ACCOUNT	SALES RETURNS AND ALLOWANCES				ACCOUNT NO. 42	
DATE		ITEM	JRNL. REF.	DEBIT	CREDIT	BALANCE

ACCOUNT	COST OF GOODS SOLD				ACCOUNT NO. 51	
DATE		ITEM	JRNL. REF.	DEBIT	CREDIT	BALANCE

P7–6A ④ ⑤

The general ledger of Katie's Supplies includes the following accounts:

Cash.................. 111	Furniture.................. 187
Inventory.............. 131	Accounts Payable........... 211
Prepaid Insurance...... 161	Rent Expense............... 564
Supplies............... 171	Utilities Expense.......... 583

Transactions in August that affected purchases and cash payments were as follows:

Aug. 1 Purchased inventory on credit from Stiples Corp., $6,900. Terms were 2/10, n/30. The invoice was dated August 1.

1 Paid monthly rent, debiting Rent Expense for $2,000.

5 Purchased supplies on credit terms of 2/10, n/30 from Bella Supply Ltd., $450. The invoice date was August 5.

8 Paid electricity bill, $600.

9 Purchased furniture on account from Rite Office Supply, $9,100. Payment terms were net 30. The invoice date was August 8.

10 Returned the furniture to Rite Office Supply. It was the wrong colour.

11 Paid Stiples Corp. the amount owed on the purchase of August 1.

12 Purchased inventory on account from Wynne Inc., $4,400. Terms were 3/10, n/30. The invoice was dated August 12.

13 Purchased inventory for cash, $650.

14 Paid a semi-annual insurance premium, debiting Prepaid Insurance, $1,200.

15 Paid the account payable to Bella Supply Ltd. from August 5.

18 Paid gas and water bills with cash, $100.

21 Purchased inventory on credit terms of 1/10, n/45 from Cyber Software Ltd., $5,200. The invoice was dated August 21.

21 Paid account payable to Wynne Inc. from August 12.

22 Purchased supplies on account from Favron Sales, $2,740. Terms were net 30. The invoice was dated August 21.

25 Returned $1,200 of the inventory purchased on August 21 to Cyber Software Ltd.

31 Paid Cyber Software Ltd. the net amount owed from August 21.

Required

1. Katie's Supplies records purchase returns in the general journal. Use the appropriate journal to record the above transactions: a purchases journal, a cash payments journal (omit the Cheque No. column), or a general journal.
2. Total each column of the special journals. Show that total debits equal total credits in each journal.
3. Show how postings would be made from the journals by writing the account numbers and check marks in the appropriate places in the journals.

Requirements 1 & 3

General Journal

DATE	ACCOUNT TITLES AND EXPLANATIONS	POST REF.	DEBIT	CREDIT

Requirements 1 – 3

Purchases Journal

PAGE

DATE	ACCOUNT CREDITED	INV. DATE	TERMS	POST. REF.	CREDITS ACCOUNTS PAYABLE	DEBITS INVENTORY	SUPPLIES	OTHER ACCOUNTS ACCOUNT TITLE	POST. REF.	AMOUNT

Requirements 1 – 3 (Continued)

Cash Payments Journal

PAGE

DATE	CHQ. NO.	ACCOUNT DEBITED	POST REF.	OTHER ACCOUNTS	ACCOUNTS PAYABLE	INVENTORY	CASH
				DEBITS		CREDITS	

P7-7A ③ ④ ⑤

Callahan Distributors, which uses the perpetual inventory system and makes all credit sales on terms of 1/10, n/30, completed the following transactions during July:

Jul. 2 Issued invoice no. 913 for sale on account to Ishikawa Inc., $24,600. Callahan's cost of this inventory was $10,800. Credit sales terms are 1/10, n/30.

3 Purchased inventory on credit terms of 3/10, n/60 from Nakkach Corp., $14,802. The invoice was dated July 3.

5 Sold inventory for cash, $6,462 (cost, $2,880).

5 Issued cheque no. 532 to purchase furniture for cash, $13,110.

8 Collected interest revenue of $6,650.

9 Issued invoice no. 914 for sale on account to Bell Ltd., $33,300 (cost, $13,860). Credit sales terms are 1/10, n/30.

10 Purchased inventory for cash, $6,858, issuing cheque no. 533.

12 Received cash from Ishikawa Inc. in full settlement of its account receivable from the sale on July 2.

13 Issued cheque no. 534 to pay Nakkach Corp. the net amount owed from July 3. (Round to the nearest dollar.)

13 Purchased supplies on account from Manley Inc., $8,646. Terms were net end of month. The invoice was dated July 13.

15 Sold inventory on account to M. O. Brown, issuing invoice no. 915 for $3,990 (cost, $1,440). Credit sales terms are 1/10, n/30.

17 Issued credit memo to M. O. Brown for $3,990 for merchandise sent in error and returned by Brown. Also accounted for receipt of the inventory.

18 Issued invoice no. 916 for credit sale to Ishikawa Inc., $2,142 (cost, $762). Credit sales terms are 1/10, n/30.

19 Received $32,967 from Bell Ltd. in full settlement of its account receivable from July 9.

20 Purchased inventory on credit terms of net 30 from Burgess Distributing Ltd., $12,282. The invoice was dated July 20.

22 Purchased furniture on credit terms of 3/10, n/60 from Nakkach Corp., $3,870. The invoice was dated July 22.

22 Issued cheque no. 535 to pay for insurance coverage, debiting Prepaid Insurance for $6,000.

24 Sold supplies to an employee for cash of $324, which was the cost of the supplies.

25 Issued cheque no. 536 to pay utilities, $6,718.

28 Purchased inventory on credit terms of 2/10, n/30 from Manley Inc., $8,050. The invoice date was July 28.

29 Returned damaged inventory to Manley Inc., issuing a debit memo for $4,050.

29 Sold goods on account to Bell Ltd., issuing invoice no. 917 for $2,976 (cost, $1,320). Credit sales terms are 1/10, n/30.

30 Issued cheque no. 537 to pay Manley Inc. $2,646.

31 Received cash in full on account from Ishikawa Inc.

31 Issued cheque no. 538 to pay monthly salaries of $14,082.

Required

(1 & 2 are completed for you)

3. Enter the transactions in a sales journal (Page 7), a cash receipts journal (Page 5), a purchases journal (Page 10), a cash payments journal (Page 8), and a general journal (Page 6), as appropriate.

4. Post daily to the accounts receivable subsidiary ledger and to the accounts payable subsidiary ledger. Post the individual amounts to the general ledger on the date recorded in the journal; post column totals to the general ledger on July 31.

5. Total each column of the special journals. Show that total debits equal total credits in each journal.

6. Balance or reconcile the accounts receivable subsidiary ledger and Accounts Receivable in the general ledger. Do the same for the accounts payable subsidiary ledger and Accounts Payable in the general ledger.

Requirements 3 & 5 (Journalizing Transactions)

Sales Journal					PAGE
DATE	INVOICE NO.	ACCOUNTS DEBITED	POST REF.	ACCOUNTS RECEIVABLE DR. SALES REVENUE CR.	COST OF GOODS SOLD DR. INVENTORY CR.

Requirements 3 & 5 (Journalizing Transactions) (Continued)

Cash Receipts Journal

PAGE

DATE	DEBITS		CREDITS					
	CASH	SALES DISCOUNTS	ACCOUNTS RECEIVABLE	SALES REVENUE	OTHER ACCOUNTS			COST OF GOODS SOLD DR. INVENTORY CR.
					ACCOUNT TITLE	POST REF.	AMOUNT	

Purchases Journal

PAGE

DATE	ACCOUNT CREDITED	INV. DATE	TERMS	POST REF.	CREDITS	DEBITS		OTHER ACCOUNTS		
					ACCOUNTS PAYABLE	INVENTORY	SUPPLIES	ACCOUNT TITLE	POST REF.	AMOUNT

Requirements 3 & 5 (Journalizing Transactions) (Continued)

Cash Payments Journal

PAGE

DATE	CHQ. NO.	PAYEE	ACCOUNT DEBITED	POST REF.	DEBITS		CREDITS	
					OTHER ACCOUNTS	ACCOUNTS PAYABLE	INVENTORY	CASH

Requirements 3 & 5 (Journalizing Transactions) (Continued)

		General Journal			PAGE
DATE		ACCOUNT TITLES AND EXPLANATIONS	POST REF.	DEBIT	CREDIT

Requirement 6

Requirement 4

Accounts Payable Subsidiary Ledger

ACCOUNT	BURGESS DISTRIBUTING LTD.				
DATE	ITEM	JRNL. REF.	DEBIT	CREDIT	BALANCE

ACCOUNT	NAKKACH CORP.				
DATE	ITEM	JRNL. REF.	DEBIT	CREDIT	BALANCE

ACCOUNT	MANLEY, INC.				
DATE	ITEM	JRNL. REF.	DEBIT	CREDIT	BALANCE

Requirement 4

General Ledger

ACCOUNT	CASH					ACCOUNT NO. 111
DATE		ITEM	JRNL. REF.	DEBIT	CREDIT	BALANCE

ACCOUNT	ACCOUNTS RECEIVABLE					ACCOUNT NO. 112
DATE		ITEM	JRNL. REF.	DEBIT	CREDIT	BALANCE

ACCOUNT	SUPPLIES					ACCOUNT NO. 116
DATE		ITEM	JRNL. REF.	DEBIT	CREDIT	BALANCE

Requirement 4 (Continued)

General Ledger

ACCOUNT	PREPAID INSURANCE				ACCOUNT NO. 117	
DATE		ITEM	JRNL. REF.	DEBIT	CREDIT	BALANCE

ACCOUNT	INVENTORY				ACCOUNT NO. 118	
DATE		ITEM	JRNL. REF.	DEBIT	CREDIT	BALANCE

ACCOUNT	FURNITURE				ACCOUNT NO. 151	
DATE		ITEM	JRNL. REF.	DEBIT	CREDIT	BALANCE

Requirement 4 (Continued)

General Ledger

ACCOUNT	ACCOUNTS PAYABLE				ACCOUNT NO. 211
DATE	ITEM	JRNL. REF.	DEBIT	CREDIT	BALANCE

ACCOUNT	SALES REVENUE				ACCOUNT NO. 411
DATE	ITEM	JRNL. REF.	DEBIT	CREDIT	BALANCE

ACCOUNT	SALES DISCOUNTS				ACCOUNT NO. 412
DATE	ITEM	JRNL. REF.	DEBIT	CREDIT	BALANCE

ACCOUNT	SALES RETURNS AND ALLOWANCES				ACCOUNT NO. 413
DATE	ITEM	JRNL. REF.	DEBIT	CREDIT	BALANCE

Requirement 4 (Continued)

General Ledger

ACCOUNT	INTEREST REVENUE				ACCOUNT NO. 419
DATE	ITEM	JRNL. REF.	DEBIT	CREDIT	BALANCE

ACCOUNT	COST OF GOODS SOLD				ACCOUNT NO. 511
DATE	ITEM	JRNL. REF.	DEBIT	CREDIT	BALANCE

ACCOUNT	SALARIES EXPENSE				ACCOUNT NO. 531
DATE	ITEM	JRNL. REF.	DEBIT	CREDIT	BALANCE

ACCOUNT	UTILITIES EXPENSE				ACCOUNT NO. 541
DATE	ITEM	JRNL. REF.	DEBIT	CREDIT	BALANCE

Requirement 4 (Continued)

Accounts Receivable Subsidiary Ledger

ACCOUNT		BELL LTD.				
DATE		ITEM	JRNL. REF.	DEBIT	CREDIT	BALANCE

ACCOUNT		M.O. BROWN				
DATE		ITEM	JRNL. REF.	DEBIT	CREDIT	BALANCE

ACCOUNT		ISHIKAWA INC.				
DATE		ITEM	JRNL. REF.	DEBIT	CREDIT	BALANCE

8 INTERNAL CONTROL AND CASH

LEARNING OBJECTIVES

1 Define internal control.
2 List and describe the components of internal control and control procedures.
3 Prepare a bank reconciliation and the related journal entries.
4 Apply internal controls to cash receipts and cash payments.
5 Apply internal controls to petty cash.
6 Make ethical business judgments.

SOME USEFUL TEXT INFORMATION (add your own notes too)

- Control procedures
- Risk assessment
- Information system   **CRIME**
- Monitoring of controls
- Environment

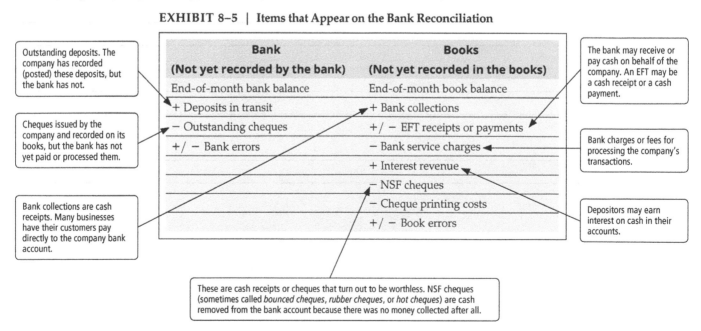

EXHIBIT 8–5 | Items that Appear on the Bank Reconciliation

Bank (Not yet recorded by the bank)	Books (Not yet recorded in the books)
End-of-month bank balance	End-of-month book balance
+ Deposits in transit	+ Bank collections
− Outstanding cheques	+/ − EFT receipts or payments
+/ − Bank errors	− Bank service charges
	+ Interest revenue
	− NSF cheques
	− Cheque printing costs
	+/ − Book errors

Outstanding deposits. The company has recorded (posted) these deposits, but the bank has not.

Cheques issued by the company and recorded on its books, but the bank has not yet paid or processed them.

Bank collections are cash receipts. Many businesses have their customers pay directly to the company bank account.

The bank may receive or pay cash on behalf of the company. An EFT may be a cash receipt or a cash payment.

Bank charges or fees for processing the company's transactions.

Depositors may earn interest on cash in their accounts.

These are cash receipts or cheques that turn out to be worthless. NSF cheques (sometimes called *bounced cheques*, *rubber cheques*, or *hot cheques*) are cash removed from the bank account because there was no money collected after all.

S8–3 ①

Explain in your own words why separation of duties is often described as the cornerstone of internal control for safeguarding assets. Describe what can happen if the same person has custody of an asset and also accounts for the asset.

_____

_____

_____

_____

_____

_____

_____

_____

_____

_____

S8–4 ②

How do external auditors differ from internal auditors? How does an external audit differ from an internal audit? How are the two types of audits similar?

_____

_____

_____

_____

_____

_____

_____

_____

_____

_____

S8–9 ③

The Cash account of Hunter Security Systems reported a balance of $4,960 at May 31, 2020. There were outstanding cheques totalling $1,800 and a May 31 deposit in transit of $400. The bank statement, which came from Royal Bank, listed a May 31 balance of $7,600. Included in the bank balance was a collection of $1,260 on account from Latha Vithanages, a Hunter customer who pays the bank directly. The bank statement also shows a $40 service charge and $20 of interest revenue that Hunter earned on its bank balance. Prepare Hunter's bank reconciliation at May 31, 2020.

	Bank Reconciliation				
Bank			Books		

S8-15 ⑤

Record the following petty cash transactions of Lexite Laminated Surfaces in general journal form (explanations are not required):

Apr. 1   Established a petty cash fund with a $200 balance.
  30   The petty cash fund has $19 in cash and $187 in petty cash tickets that were issued to pay for office supplies ($117) and entertainment expenses ($70). Replenished the fund with $181 of cash and recorded the expenses.

		General Journal			
DATE		ACCOUNT TITLES AND EXPLANATIONS	POST REF.	DEBIT	CREDIT

S8-16 ⑥

Angela Brennan, an accountant for Dublin Co., discovers that her supervisor, Barney Stone, made several errors last year. Overall, the errors overstated the company's net income by 15 percent. It is not clear whether the errors were deliberate or accidental. What should Brennan do?

E8–8 ③

The following items could appear on a bank reconciliation:

a. Outstanding cheques

b. Deposits in transit for current month

c. NSF cheque

d. Bank collection of a note receivable on the company's behalf

e. Bank credit memo for interest earned on bank balance

f. Bank debit memo for service charge

g. Book error: We credited Cash for $200. The correct credit was $2,000.

h. Bank error: The bank decreased our account for a cheque written by another customer.

i. Outstanding cheques from the previous month that are still outstanding

j. EFT payment by a customer

k. Bank error in recording a deposit for $464 should have been $446

Required

1. Classify each item as (1) an addition to the book balance, (2) a subtraction from the book balance, (3) an addition to the bank balance, or (4) a subtraction from the bank balance.

2. Indicate (a) the items that will result in an adjustment to the company's records, and (b) why the other items do not require an adjustment.

Requirements 1 & 2a

	Classification of Change (1,2,3, or 4)	Adjustment Required (Y/N)
a.	4	
b.	3	
c.	2	
d.	1	
e.	1	
f.	2	
g.	2	
h.		N
i.		
j.		
k.		

Requirement 2b

E8–9   ③

Adams Enterprises began operations on January 2, 2020, depositing $40,000 in the bank. During this first month of business, the following transactions occurred that affected the Cash account in the general ledger:

Date	Description	Dr	Cr
Jan. 2	Deposit	$40,000	
5	Payment, cheque 001		$12,000
8	Payment, cheque 002		16,000
9	Cash sales	16,000	
15	Payment, cheque 003		10,000
18	Cash sales	12,000	
20	Bank loan	50,000	
26	Equipment purchase, cheque 004		74,000
30	Payment on account, cheque 005		17,000
31	Cash sales	25,600	

Shortly after the end of January the company received its first bank statement:

BANK STATEMENT FOR JANUARY 2020

Description	Withdrawals	Deposits	Date	Balance
Balance Forward			Jan01	0
Deposit		40,000	Jan02	40,000
Chq#001	12,000		Jan07	28,000
Deposit		16,000	Jan09	44,000
Chq#002	16,000		Jan13	28,000
Deposit		12,000	Jan18	40,000
Bank Loan		50,000	Jan20	90,000
Chq#004	74,000		Jan28	16,000
Deposit		2,000	Jan29	18,000
Service Charge	48		Jan31	17,952
Interest		8	Jan31	17,960
	102,048	120,008		

In preparing to do the bank reconciliation, Adams Enterprises noticed that the $2,000 deposit on January 29 was a bank error and informed the bank. The bank will correct the error on the next bank statement.

Required Prepare Adams Enterprises' bank reconciliation at January 31, 2020.

Bank Reconciliation		
Bank		
Books		

F8–10 ③

Padilha Rental Company's general ledger Cash account showed the following transactions during October 2020:

Date		Description	Dr	Cr	Balance
Oct.	1	Opening balance			$ 2,800
	2	Deposit	$20,000		22,800
	5	Payment, cheque 233		$ 6,000	16,800
	8	Payment, cheque 234		18,000	(1,200)
	9	Deposit	18,000		16,800
	15	Payment, cheque 235		5,000	11,800
	18	Deposit	5,200		17,000
	26	Payment, cheque 236		3,300	13,700
	30	Payment, cheque 237		4,750	8,950
	31	Deposit	10,500		19,450

The bank statement for the month ending October 31, 2020, is shown below:

BANK STATEMENT FOR OCTOBER 2020

Description	Withdrawals	Deposits	Date	Balance
Balance Forward			Oct01	2,800
Deposit		20,000	Oct02	22,800
Chq#00233	6,000		Oct07	16,800
Deposit		18,000	Oct09	34,800
Chq#00234	18,000		Oct10	16,800
Deposit		5,200	Oct18	22,000
Chq#00235	5,000		Oct18	17,000
Service Charge	120		Oct31	16,880
Service Charge	120		Oct31	16,760
Interest		4	Oct31	16,764
	29,240	43,204		

Padhila Rental Company informed its bank that the bank charged a service charge twice. The bank has agreed to reverse one of the bank charges on the next month's bank statement.

Required Prepare Padhila Rental Company's bank reconciliation at October 31, 2020.

Bank Reconciliation		

E8–15 ④

When you pay for goods at La Tienda Foods, the cash register displays the amount of the sale, the cash received, and any change returned to you. Suppose the register also produces a customer receipt but keeps no record of the sales transactions. At the end of the day, the clerk counts the cash in the register and gives it to the cashier for deposit in the company bank account.

Required Write a memo to Mia Francesca, the owner. Identify the internal control weakness over cash receipts, and explain how the weakness gives an employee the opportunity to steal cash. State how to prevent such a theft.

E8–16 ④

Gary's Motors purchases high-performance auto parts from a Winnipeg vendor. Joel Sieben, the accountant for Gary's, verifies receipt of merchandise and then prepares, signs, and mails the cheque to the vendor.

Required

1. Identify the internal control weakness over cash payments in this scenario.
2. What could the business do to correct the weakness?

E8–18 ⑤

The petty cash fund had the following petty cash tickets:

Toner for a printer..	$ 42
Freight to deliver goods sold..............................	39
Freight on inventory purchased.........................	112
Miscellaneous expense...	10
Postage expense..	25
	$228

Assume that the business has established a petty cash fund in the amount of $250 and that the amount of cash in the fund at the time of replenishment is $20. The business uses a perpetual inventory system.

Prepare the entry to replenish the fund on February 28.

Calculations:

	General Journal			
DATE	ACCOUNT TITLES AND EXPLANATIONS	POST REF.	DEBIT	CREDIT

E8-19 ⑤

Record the following selected transactions of Kelly's Organics in general journal format (explanations are not required):

Jun. 1   Established a petty cash fund with a $200 balance.

2   Journalized the day's cash sales. Cash register tapes show a $4,875 total, but the cash in the register is $4,885.

10   The petty cash fund had $56.50 in cash and $134.00 in petty cash tickets issued to pay for office supplies ($21.00), delivery expenses ($69.50), and entertainment expenses ($43.50). Replenished the fund.

Calculations:

General Journal

DATE		ACCOUNT TITLES AND EXPLANATIONS	POST REF.	DEBIT	CREDIT

E8–21 ⑤

Maritime Distributors created a $500 imprest petty cash fund on September 7 with the expectation that when the balance reached below $100, it would be replenished. During the first few weeks of use, the fund custodian authorized and signed petty cash tickets as shown below.

Date	Ticket No.	Item	Account Debited	Amount
Sep. 8	1	Delivery of flyers to customers	Delivery Expense	$228.80
Sep. 22	2	Stamp purchase	Postage Expense	85.98
Sep. 29	3	Newsletter	Supplies Expense	60.40
Oct. 3	4	Key to closet	Miscellaneous Expense	9.52
Oct. 13	5	Staples	Supplies Expense	14.72

Required Make general journal entries to (a) create the petty cash fund and (b) record its replenishment at October 15. Cash in the fund totals $97.58. Include explanations.

General Journal

DATE	ACCOUNT TITLES AND EXPLANATIONS	POST REF.	DEBIT	CREDIT

E8–22 ⑤

Refer to the Maritime Distributors petty cash fund data in E8–21. Suppose, one month later, on November 15, the company decided to decrease the petty cash fund by $100 due to theft and break-ins in the area. Journalize the decrease in the petty cash fund.

General Journal

DATE	ACCOUNT TITLES AND EXPLANATIONS	POST REF.	DEBIT	CREDIT

E8–25 ③ Serial Exercise

The Serial Exercise involves a company that will be revisited throughout relevant chapters in Volume 1 and Volume 2. You can complete the Serial Exercises using MyLab Accounting.

This exercise continues recordkeeping for the Canyon Canoe Company. You can do this question even if you have not completed prior questions from this series.

Canyon Canoe Company has decided to open a new chequing account at River Nations Bank during March 2021. Canyon Canoe Company's March Cash T-account for the new cash account from its general ledger is as follows:

Cash—River Nations Bank Chequing Account

Mar.	1	Bal.	0	200	Mar.	2	Chq#101
	2	Deposit	10,000	4,300		4	Chq#102
	13	Deposit	2,325	750		9	Chq#103
	20	Deposit	2,750	1,675		14	Chq#104
	27	Deposit	4,500	1,500		21	Chq#105
	31	Deposit	3,490	175		28	Chq#106
				300		30	Chq#107
		Bal.	14,165				

Canyon Canoe Company's bank statement dated March 31, 2021, follows:

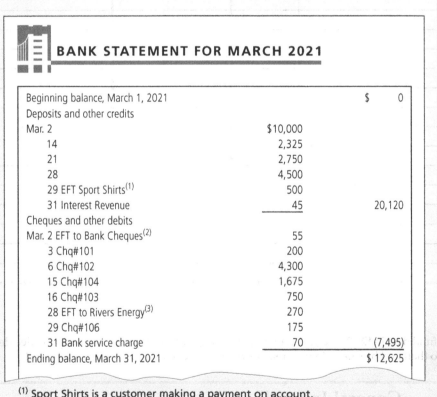

BANK STATEMENT FOR MARCH 2021

Beginning balance, March 1, 2021		$ 0
Deposits and other credits		
Mar. 2	$10,000	
14	2,325	
21	2,750	
28	4,500	
29 EFT Sport Shirts[1]	500	
31 Interest Revenue	45	20,120
Cheques and other debits		
Mar. 2 EFT to Bank Cheques[2]	55	
3 Chq#101	200	
6 Chq#102	4,300	
15 Chq#104	1,675	
16 Chq#103	750	
28 EFT to Rivers Energy[3]	270	
29 Chq#106	175	
31 Bank service charge	70	(7,495)
Ending balance, March 31, 2021		$ 12,625

[1] Sport Shirts is a customer making a payment on account.
[2] Bank Cheques is a company that prints business cheques (Use the Bank Charges Expense account.)
[3] Rivers Energy is a utility provider.

Required

1. Prepare the bank reconciliation at March 31, 2021.

2. Journalize any transactions required from the bank reconciliation.

3. Compute the adjusted account balance for the Cash T-account, and denote the balance as *Bal.* Does the adjusted balance of the Cash T-account match the adjusted book balance on the bank reconciliation?

Requirement 1

Requirement 2

General Journal

DATE		ACCOUNT TITLES AND EXPLANATIONS	POST REF.	DEBIT	CREDIT

Requirement 3

Cash—River Nations Bank Chequing Account

Mar. 1	0	Mar. 2	200
Mar. 2	10,000	Mar. 4	4,300
Mar. 13	2,325	Mar. 9	750
Mar. 20	2,750	Mar. 14	1,675
Mar. 27	4,500	Mar. 21	1,500
Mar. 31	3,490	Mar. 28	175
		Mar. 30	300
Bal.	14,165		

P8–3A ②

Each of the following situations has an internal control weakness:

a. Syspro Software Associates sells accounting software. Recently, the development of a new software program stopped while the programmers redesigned Syspro Software Associates' accounting system. Syspro Software Associates' own accountants could have performed this task.

b. Judy Sloan has been your trusted employee for 30 years. She performs all cash-handling and accounting duties. She has just purchased a new Lexus and a new home in an expensive suburb. As the owner of the company, you wonder how she can afford these luxuries because you pay her $35,000 per year and she has no sources of outside income.

c. Sanchez Hardwoods Ltd., a private corporation, falsified sales and inventory figures to get a large loan. The company prepared its own financial statements. The company received the loan but later went bankrupt and couldn't repay the loan.

d. The office supply company from which The Family Shoe Store purchases sales receipts recently notified Family that the last shipped receipts were not prenumbered. Louise Bourseault, the owner of Family, replied that she never uses the receipt numbers, so the omission is not important.

e. Discount stores such as Dollar Mart make most of their sales for cash, with the remainder in debit card and credit card sales. To reduce expenses, one store manager ceases purchasing fidelity bonds on the cashiers.

Required

1. Identify the missing internal control characteristic in each situation.
2. Identify the potential problem that could be caused by each control weakness.
3. Propose a solution to each internal control problem.

MISSING INTERNAL CONTROL CHARACTERSTIC	POSSIBLE PROBLEM	SOLUTION

P8–4A ③

The cash receipts and the cash payments of Spinners Bowling for November 2020 are as follows:

Cash Receipts (Posting Reference is CR)			**Cash Payments (Posting Reference is CP)**	
Date	**Cash Debit**		**Cheque No.**	**Cash Credit**
Nov. 5	$ 3,436		1221	$ 1,819
7	470		1222	1,144
13	1,723		1223	429
15	1,065		1224	111
19	441		1225	816
24	10,875		1226	109
30	2,598		1227	4,468
Total	$20,608		1228	998
			1229	330
			1230	2,724
			Total	$12,948

The Cash account of Spinners Bowling shows a balance of $26,983 on November 30, 2020. Outstanding amounts from the previous month's bank reconciliation were cheque #1219 for $500, cheque #1218 for $400, and an October 31 deposit in the amount of $2,000. On December 3, 2020, Spinners Bowling received this bank statement:

BANK STATEMENT FOR NOVEMBER 2020

Description	Withdrawals	Deposits	Date	Balance
Balance Forward			Nov01	18,223
Deposit		2,000	Nov01	20,223
EFT Rent Collection		880	Nov01	21,103
Deposit		3,436	Nov06	24,539
NSF Cheque	433		Nov08	24,106
Chq#001221	1,819		Nov09	22,287
Deposit		470	Nov10	22,757
Chq#001222	1,144		Nov13	21,613
Chq#001223	429		Nov14	21,184
Deposit		1,723	Nov14	22,907
Chq#001224	111		Nov15	22,796
Deposit		1,065	Nov15	23,861
EFT Insurance	275		Nov19	23,586
Deposit		441	Nov20	24,027
Chq#001225	816		Nov22	23,211
Deposit		10,875	Nov25	34,086
Chq#001226	109		Nov29	33,977
Chq#001227	4,968		Nov30	29,009
Bank Collection		1,430	Nov30	30,439
Chq#001219	500		Nov30	29,939
Service Charge	25		Nov30	29,914
	10,629	22,320		

Explanations: EFT—electronic funds transfer, NSF—nonsufficient funds

Additional data for the bank reconciliation is as follows:

a. The EFT deposit was a receipt of monthly rent. The EFT debit was payment for monthly insurance.

b. The NSF cheque was received late in October from a customer.

c. The $1,430 bank collection of a note receivable on November 30 included $100 interest revenue.

d. The correct amount of cheque #1227, a payment on account, is $4,968. (Spinner Bowling's accountant mistakenly recorded the cheque for $4,468.)

Required

1. Prepare the bank reconciliation of Spinners Bowling at November 30, 2020.

2. Describe how a bank account and the bank reconciliation help Spinners Bowling's managers control the business's cash.

3. How are outstanding items from the previous month's bank reconciliation that clear on the November bank statement dealt with?

Requirement 1

Requirements 2 & 3

_____

_____

_____

_____

_____

_____

P8–5A

Spottify Electronics had a computer failure on October 1, 2020, that resulted in the loss of data, including the balance of its Cash account and its bank reconciliation from September 30, 2020. The accountant, Crisanto Danila, has been able to obtain the following information from the records of the company and its bank:

a. An examination showed that two cheques (#244 for $305.00 and #266 for $632.50) had not been cashed as of October 1. Danila recalled that there was only one deposit in transit on the September 30 bank reconciliation but was unable to recall the amount.

b. The cash receipts and cash payments journals contained the following entries for October 2020:

Cash Receipts	Cash Payments	
Amounts	**Cheque No.**	**Amount**
$ 908.50	275	$ 310.50
1,748.00	276	448.50
3,726.00	277	466.90
1,975.00	278	811.90
736.00	279	577.30
$9,093.50	280	3,886.90
	281	void
	282	488.50
	283	1,058.00
		$8,048.50

c. The company's bank provided the following statement as of October 31, 2020:

BANK STATEMENT FOR OCTOBER 2020

Date	Cheques and Other Debits		Deposits and Other Credits		Balance
Oct. 1	#276	448.50		2,346.00	6,520.50
2	#266	632.50			5,888.00
5	#277	466.90			5,421.10
8				908.50	6,329.60
14	#275	310.50		1,196.00	7,215.10
17	EFT	529.00			6,686.10
19			EFT	414.00	7,100.10
22	#279	577.30		1,748.00	8,270.80
22	#280	3,976.90	EFT	1,196.00	5,489.90
24			EFT	471.50	5,961.40
27	NSF	805.00		3,726.00	8,882.40
28	SC	20.00			8,862.40
31	#283	1,058.00		1,975.00	9,779.40

d. The deposit made on October 14 was for the collection of a note receivable ($1,100.00) plus interest.

e. The electronic funds transfers (EFTs) had not yet been recorded by Spottify Electronics because the bank statement was the first notification of them.

- The October 17 EFT was for the monthly payment on an insurance policy for Spottify Electronics.
- The October 19 and 24 EFTs were collections on accounts receivable.
- The October 22 EFT was in error—the transfer should have been to the Spottify Horse Farm.

f. The NSF cheque on October 27 was received from a customer as payment for electronics purchased for $805.00.

g. Cheque #280 was correctly written for $3,976.90 for the purchase of inventory (assume a periodic system) but incorrectly recorded by the cash payments clerk.

Required

1. Prepare a bank reconciliation as of October 31, 2020, including the calculation of the book balance of October 31, 2020.
2. Prepare all journal entries that would be required by the bank reconciliation. No explanations are needed.

Requirement 1

Requirement 2

General Journal

DATE		ACCOUNT TITLES AND EXPLANATIONS	POST REF.	DEBIT	CREDIT

P8–9A (5)

Suppose that, on June 1, Devine Design creates a petty cash fund with an imprest balance of $400. During June, Lucie Chao, the fund custodian, signs the following petty cash tickets:

Ticket No.	Item	Amount
101	Office supplies	$ 26.64
102	Cab fare for executive	60.00
103	Delivery of package across town	29.32
104	Dinner money for sales manager entertaining a customer	133.34
105	Office supplies	127.20

On June 30, prior to replenishment, the fund contains these tickets plus $34.40. The accounts affected by petty cash payments are Office Supplies Expense, Travel Expense, Delivery Expense, and Entertainment Expense.

Required

1. Explain the characteristics and internal control features of an imprest fund.
2. On June 30, how much cash should the petty cash fund hold before it is replenished?
3. Make general journal entries to (a) create the fund and (b) replenish it. Include explanations.
4. Make the July 1 entry to increase the fund balance to $500. Include an explanation, and briefly describe what the custodian does in this case.

Requirements 1 & 2

Requirements 3 and 4

DATE	ACCOUNT TITLES AND EXPLANATIONS	POST REF.	DEBIT	CREDIT

General Journal

9 RECEIVABLES

LEARNING OBJECTIVES

1 Define common types of receivables, and report receivables on the balance sheet.
2 Use the allowance method to account for uncollectibles, and estimate uncollectibles by the percent-of-sales, aging-of-accounts-receivable, and the percent-of-accounts receivable methods.
3 Use the direct write-off method to account for uncollectibles.
4 Account for credit card, debit card, and online sales.
5 Account for notes receivable.
6 Use the acid-test ratio and days' sales in receivables to evaluate a company.
7 Understand the impact on accounts receivable of International Financial Reporting Standards (IFRS).

*A1 Discount a note receivable.

SOME USEFUL TEXT INFORMATION (add your own notes too)

> **Percent-of-Sales Method:**
> Bad Debt Expense = Net credit sales × estimated%

> **Percent-of-Accounts-Receivable Method:**
>
> Target Allowance Balance = Accounts Receivable Balance × estimated %
> Bad Debts Expense = Target Allowance Balance − Actual Allowance Balance

EXHIBIT 9–3 | Comparing the Allowance Methods for Estimating Uncollectibles

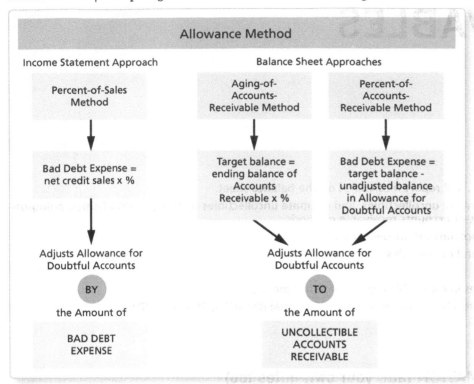

Accounts Receivable		Allowance for Doubtful Accounts	
1. Sales on credit	2. Customer payments on account		3. Estimate of uncollectible
	4. Write off uncollectible	4. Write off uncollectible	
5. Recovery of account reinstated			5. Recovery of account reinstated

$$\text{Amount of simple interest} = \text{Principal} \times \text{Interest rate} \times \text{Time}$$

$$\text{Acid-test ratio} = \frac{\text{Cash} + \text{Short-term investments} + \text{Net current receivables}}{\text{Total current liabilities}}$$

$$\text{Days' sales in receivables} = \frac{\text{Average net accounts receivable}}{\text{One days' sales}} = \frac{\left(\dfrac{\text{Beginning net receivables}}{+ \text{ Ending net receivables}}\right) \div 2}{\text{One day's sales}}$$

$$\text{Account receivable turnover} = \frac{\text{Net credit sales}}{\text{Average net accounts receivable}}$$

S9–7 ②

University Cycle Shop had trouble collecting its account receivable from Matt Reid. On January 19, University finally wrote off Reid's $2,400 account receivable. University turned the account over to a lawyer, who pursued Reid for payment for the rest of the year. On December 31, Reid sent a $2,400 cheque to University Cycle Shop with a note that said, "Here's your money. Please call off your bloodhound!"

Journalize the following transactions for University Cycle Shop:

Jan. 19 Write-off of Reid's account against Allowance for Doubtful Accounts.
Dec. 31 Reinstatement of Reid's account.
31 Collection of cash from Reid.

\ General Journal					
DATE		ACCOUNT TITLES AND EXPLANATIONS	POST REF.	DEBIT	CREDIT

S9–8 ②

Tolco Importers Inc. had the following balances at the end of the year, before the year-end adjustments:

Accounts Receivable	Allowance for Doubtful Accounts
148,000	4,000

The aging of accounts receivable yields these data:

	A	B	C	D
1		Age of Accounts Receivable		
2		0–60 Days	Over 60 Days	Total Receivables
3	Accounts receivable	$140,000	$8,000	$148,000
4	Percent uncollectible	3%	20%	

1. Journalize Tolco Importers Inc.'s entry to adjust the Allowance account to its correct balance at year end.
2. Prepare the T-account for Allowance for Doubtful Accounts.
3. Repeat question 1 assuming that, instead of aging the accounts, the allowance is calculated as 3.5 percent of the Accounts Receivable balance.

Requirement 1

General Journal

DATE	ACCOUNT TITLES AND EXPLANATIONS	POST REF.	DEBIT	CREDIT

Requirement 2

Allowance for Doubtful Accounts

Requirement 3

General Journal

DATE	ACCOUNT TITLES AND EXPLANATIONS	POST REF.	DEBIT	CREDIT

S9–9 ③

Branson Shipping uses the direct write-off method in dealing with uncollectible accounts because it is highly unusual that the business ever has bad debts, and when they do they are not material in relation to total sales.

2019

Oct. 15   Shipped goods for Marine Specialties on account, $2,200.

2020

May 15   Received notice of bankruptcy from Marine Specialties and wrote off the amount they owed from the October 15 sale.

1. Journalize the transactions.
2. What is the major flaw in using the direct write-off method as opposed to the allowance method?

DATE	ACCOUNT TITLES AND EXPLANATIONS	POST REF.	DEBIT	CREDIT
General Journal				

S9–12 ④

Northern Consultants accepts American Express credit cards from its customers. Assume Northern makes a sale of $2,000 and the credit card company charges a 3 percent fee. Provide the journal entry on June 22 to record the sales revenue.

DATE	ACCOUNT TITLES AND EXPLANATIONS	POST REF.	DEBIT	CREDIT
General Journal				

S9-15 ⑤

For each of the following notes receivable, compute the amount of interest revenue earned during 2020. Use a 365-day year or base your calculations on the number of months, depending on how the interest period is stated, and round only your answer to the nearest dollar.

	Principal	Interest Rate	Interest Period During 2020
Note 1	$200,000	8%	6 months
Note 2	30,000	4	75 days
Note 3	20,000	9	60 days
Note 4	100,000	5	3 months

S9-20 ⑦

In determining how accounts should be presented, accountants are concerned about the values being both relevant and reliable. Is the accounts receivable value presented on the balance sheet both relevant and reliable under IFRS?

E9-1 ①

From the following list of adjusted account balances, prepare the current asset section of Delainey's Hardscaping for December 31, 2020. Assume all accounts have normal balances.

Accounts receivable	$51,000	Inventory	$22,000
Bad debt expense	1,200	Cash	15,000
Notes receivable, due August 31, 2021	12,000	Accumulated Amortization-Equipment	5,000
Supplies	1,440	Allowance for doubtful accounts	3,500
Notes receivable, due August 31, 2023	5,300	Equipment	25,000

②

On February 28, Big White Ski Equipment had a $25,500 debit balance in Accounts Receivable. During March, the company had sales of $65,500, which included $60,000 in credit sales. March collections were $53,000, and write-offs of uncollectible receivables totalled $1,250. Other data include:

a. February 28 credit balance in Allowance for Doubtful Accounts is $1,300.

b. Bad debt expense is estimated as 3 percent of credit sales.

Required

1. Prepare journal entries to record sales, collections, write-offs of uncollectibles during March, and bad debt expense by the allowance method (using the percent-of-sales method). Use March 31 as the journal entry date. Explanations are not required.

2. Prepare T-accounts to show the ending balances in Accounts Receivable and Allowance for Doubtful Accounts. Compute *net* Accounts Receivable at March 31. How much does Big White expect to collect?

Requirement 1

\multicolumn{6}{c}{**General Journal**}
DATE		ACCOUNT TITLES AND EXPLANATIONS	POST REF.	DEBIT	CREDIT

Requirement 2

Accounts Receivable	Allowance for Doubtful Accounts

E9–4 ②

Lui Dental began operations in January 2020 selling dental appliances to dentists. The following transactions occurred during the first six months of operations:

Jan. 15   Sold appliances to Dr. Hall on account for $15,750; cost $6,400.

Feb. 22   Received payment in full from Dr. Hall.

Mar. 4   Sold merchandise to Dr. Evans on account for $4,400; cost $1,250.

Apr. 20   Sold merchandise to Dr. Murray on account for $6,700; cost $2,990.

May 31   Sold merchandise to Dr. Kim on account for $3,200; cost $1,100.

Jun. 28   Received $3,000 on account from Dr. Evans.

Required

1. Complete the following aged listing of customer accounts as of June 30, 2020:

	A	B	C	D	E	F
1		Age of Accounts Receivable				
2	Customer	1–30 Days	31–60 Days	61–90 Days	Over 90 Days	Total
3	Dr. Evans					
4	Dr. Hall					
5	Dr. Kim	3,200				3,200
6	Dr. Murray					
7	Totals:					

2. Estimate the Allowance for Doubtful Accounts required at June 30, 2020, assuming the following uncollectible rates: 30 days, 2%; 60 days, 5%; 90 days, 15%; > 90 days, 50%. Hint: use the above chart totals.

3. Show how Lui Dental would report its accounts receivable on its June 30, 2020, balance sheet. What amounts would be reported on an income statement prepared for the six-month period ended June 30, 2020?

4. If Dr. Evans's account needed to be written off in September 2020, how accurate is Lui Dental at estimating its bad debts?

Requirement 3

Requirement 4

E9-9 ④

Record the following transactions in the general journal of Jesse's Quick Clean Service. Assume Scotiabank charges merchants $0.50 per debit card transaction and MasterCard charges 4 percent of sales as service fees.

Mar. 31   Scotiabank debit card sales of $22,000, consisting of 1,500 transactions.

     31   MasterCard credit card sales of $33,000.

Mar. 31   FleetPlan card accepted for $2,800 of payments. This card requires that receipts are submitted for payment manually. A 2 percent fee applies.

Apr. 10   Payment was received from FleetPlan.

		General Journal			
DATE		ACCOUNT TITLES AND EXPLANATIONS	POST REF.	DEBIT	CREDIT

E9–11 ⑤

Tropical North Company, which has a December 31 year end and uses a periodic inventory system, completed the following transactions during 2019 and 2020:

2019

Oct. 14 Sold merchandise to OFTR Racing, receiving a 60-day, 6 percent note for $5,000.

Nov. 16 Sold merchandise to Sunshine Racing receiving a 72-day, 4 percent note for $7,500.

Dec. 13 Received amount due from OFTR Racing.

Dec. 31 Accrued interest on the Sunshine Racing note.

2020

Jan. 27 Collected in full from Sunshine Company.

Required Prepare the necessary journal entries to record the above transactions. Assume that a 365-day year is used for calculations.

\multicolumn{5}{c}{General Journal}
DATE	ACCOUNT TITLES AND EXPLANATIONS	POST REF.	DEBIT	CREDIT

E9–14 ⑥

Vision Electronics, which makes DVD players, reported the following items at February 28, 2020 (amounts in thousands, with last year's—2019—amounts also given as needed):

Accounts Payable...................	$1,796	Accounts Receivable, net	
Cash..	860	February 29, 2020	$ 440
Inventories		February 28, 2019	300
February 29, 2020	380	Cost of Goods Sold............................	4,800
February 28, 2019	320	Short-term Investments....................	330
Net Sales Revenue..................	7,720	Other Current Assets	180
Long-term Assets	820	Other Current Liabilities..................	290
Long-term Liabilities	20		

Compute for 2020 Vision Electronics' (a) acid-test ratio, (b) days' sales in average receivables, (c) current ratio, (d) debt ratio, (e) gross margin percent, (f) inventory turnover. Evaluate each ratio value as strong or weak. Assume Vision Electronics sells on terms of net 30.

a. Acid-test ratio

b. Days' sales in average receivables

c. Current ratio

d. Debt ratio

e. Gross margin percentage

f. Rate of inventory

E9-15 ⑥

Franklin Ltd., a gift store, reported the following amounts in its 2020 financial statements. The 2019 figures are given for comparison.

		2020		2019	
Current assets					
Cash		$ 12,000			$ 26,000
Short-term investments		46,000			22,000
Accounts receivable	$120,000		$148,000		
Less: Allow. for doubtful accts	20,000	100,000	18,000		130,000
Inventory		384,000			378,000
Prepaid insurance		4,000			4,000
Total current assets		$ 546,000			$ 560,000
Total current liabilities		$ 218,000			$ 224,000
Net sales		$1,460,000			$1,464,000

Required

1. Determine whether Franklin Ltd.'s acid-test ratio improved or deteriorated from 2019 to 2020. How does Franklin Ltd.'s acid-test ratio compare with the industry average of 0.90?

2. Compare the days' sales in receivables measure for 2020 with the company's credit terms of net 30. What action, if any, should Franklin Ltd. take?

3. Indicate the most likely effect of the following changes in credit policy on the days' sales in receivables (+ for increase, − for decrease, and NE for no effect):

   a. Granted credit to people with poor credit history.

   b. Increased collection techniques or methods.

   c. Granted credit with discounts for early payment.

Requirements 1 & 2

_____

_____

_____

_____

_____

_____

_____

_____

_____

_____

_____

_____

Requirements 1 & 2 (Continued)

_____
_____
_____
_____
_____
_____
_____
_____
_____
_____
_____
_____
_____
_____
_____
_____
_____
_____
_____
_____
_____
_____

Calculations:

Requirement 3

a. _____
b. _____
c. _____

E9-20 ② — Serial Exercise

The Serial Exercise involves a company that will be revisited throughout relevant chapters in Volume 1 and Volume 2. You can complete the Serial Exercises using MyLab Accounting.

This exercise continues recordkeeping for the Canyon Canoe Company. Students do not have to complete prior exercises in order to answer this exercise.

Canyon Canoe Company has experienced rapid growth in its first few months of operations and has had a significant increase in customers renting canoes and purchasing T-shirts. Many of these customers are asking for credit terms. Amber Wilson, owner and company manager, has decided it is time to review the business transactions and update some of the business practices. Her first step is to make decisions about handling accounts receivable. So far, year-to-date credit sales have been $15,500. A review of outstanding receivables resulted in the following aging schedule:

	A	B	C	D	E	F
1	**Age of Accounts as of June 30, 2021**					
2	**Customer Name**	**1–30 Days**	**31–60 Days**	**61–90 Days**	**Over 90 Days**	**Total**
3	Canyon Youth Club	$ 250				$ 250
4	Crazy Tees	200	$150			350
5	Early Start Daycare				$500	500
6	Lakefront Pavilion	575				575
7	Outdoor Center			$300		300
8	Rivers Canoe Club	350				350
9	Sport Shirts	450	120			570
10	Zack's Marina	75	75	75		225
11	Totals	$1,900	$345	$375	$500	$3,120

Required

1. The company wants to use the allowance method to estimate bad debts. Determine the estimated bad debts expense under the following methods at June 30, 2021. Assume a zero beginning balance for Allowance for Doubtful Accounts. Round to the nearest dollar.

   a. Percent-of-sales method, assuming 4.5% of credit sales will not be collected.

   b. Percent-of-receivables method, assuming 22.5% of receivables will not be collected.

   c. Aging-of-receivables method, assuming 5% of invoices 1–30 days will not be collected, 20% of invoices 31–60 days, 40% of invoices 61–90 days, and 75% of invoices over 90 days.

2. Journalize the entry at June 30, 2021, to adjust for bad debts expense using the percent-of-sales method.

3. Journalize the entry at June 30, 2021, to record the write-off of the Early Start Daycare invoice.

4. At June 30, 2021, open T-accounts for Accounts Receivable and Allowance for Doubtful Accounts before requirements 2 and 3. Post entries from requirements 2 and 3 to those accounts. Assume a zero beginning balance for Allowance for Doubtful Accounts.

5. Show how Canyon Canoe Company will report net accounts receivable on the balance sheet on June 30, 2021.

Requirement 1

1a. Percent-of-sales method:

1b. Percent-of-accounts-receivable method:

1c. Aging-of-accounts-receivable method:

Age of Accounts as of June 30, 2021					
Customer Name	**1–30 Days**	**31–60 Days**	**61–90 Days**	**Over 90 Days**	**Total Balance**
Totals					
Estimated percent uncollectible					
Allowance for doubtful accounts					

_____

_____

_____

_____

_____

_____

Requirements 2 and 3

General Journal				
DATE	ACCOUNT TITLES AND EXPLANATIONS	POST REF.	DEBIT	CREDIT

Requirement 4

Accounts Receivable	Allowance for Doubtful Accounts

Requirement 5

CANYON CANOE COMPANY		
Balance Sheet (partial)		
June 30, 2021		

Journal

DATE		ACCOUNT TITLES AND EXPLANATIONS	POST REF.	DEBIT	CREDIT

P9–2A ②

Matiere Co. completed the following transactions during 2019 and 2020:

2019

Dec. 31 Estimated that bad debt expense for the year was 3 percent of credit sales of $385,000 and recorded that amount as expense.

31 Made the closing entry for bad debt expense.

2020

Mar. 26 Sold inventory to Mabel Sanders, $10,037.50, on credit terms of 2/10, n/30. Ignore cost of goods sold.

Sep. 15 Wrote off Mabel Sanders's account as uncollectible after repeated efforts to collect from her.

Nov. 10 Received $5,500 from Sanders, along with a letter stating her intention to pay her debt in full within 30 days. Reinstated her account in full.

Dec. 5 Received the balance due from Sanders.

31 Made a compound entry to write off the following accounts as uncollectible: Curt Major, $2,200; Bernadette Lalonde, $962.50; Ellen Smart, $1,470.

31 Estimated that bad debt expense for the year was 2 percent of credit sales of $490,000 and recorded the expense.

31 Made the closing entry for bad debt expense.

Matiere records all amounts to the nearest cent. Present all amounts to two decimal places.

Required

1. Open three-column general ledger accounts for Allowance for Doubtful Accounts and Bad Debt Expense. Keep running balances.

2. Record the transactions in the general journal and post to the ledger accounts.

3. The December 31, 2020, balance of Accounts Receivable is $146,000. Show how Accounts Receivable would be reported at that date.

4. Assume that Matiere Co. begins aging accounts receivable on December 31, 2020. The balance in Accounts Receivable is $146,000, the credit balance in Allowance for Doubtful Accounts is $16,717.50 (use your calculations from Requirement 3), and the company estimates that $19,900 of its accounts receivable will prove uncollectible.

   a. Make the adjusting entry for uncollectibles.

   b. Show how Accounts Receivable will be reported on the December 31, 2020, balance sheet after this adjusting entry.

Requirements 1 & 2

General Journal

DATE		ACCOUNT TITLES AND EXPLANATIONS	POST REF.	DEBIT	CREDIT

Requirements 1 and 2

ACCOUNT: ALLOWANCE FOR DOUBTFUL ACCOUNTS					
DATE	ITEM	JRNL. REF	DEBIT	CREDIT	BALANCE

ACCOUNT: BAD DEBT EXPENSE					
DATE	ITEM	JRNL. REF.	DEBIT	CREDIT	BALANCE

Requirement 3

Requirement 4a

General Journal				
DATE	ACCOUNT TITLES AND EXPLANATIONS	POST REF.	DEBIT	CREDIT

Requirement 4b

P9–4A ② ③

On March 31, 2020, Summitt Manufacturing had a $290,000 debit balance in Accounts Receivable. During April, the business had sales revenue of $1,150,000, which included $990,000 in credit sales. Other data for April include the following:

a. Collections on accounts receivable, $910,000.

b. Write-offs of uncollectible receivables, $4,500.

Required

1. Record bad debt expense for April by the direct write-off method. Use T-accounts to show all April activity in Accounts Receivable and Bad Debt Expense.

2. Record bad debt expense and write-offs of customer accounts for April by the allowance method. Use T-accounts to show all April activity in Accounts Receivable, Allowance for Doubtful Accounts, and Bad Debt Expense. The March 31 unadjusted balance in Allowance for Doubtful Accounts was $1,200 (debit). Bad debt expense was estimated at 1 percent of credit sales.

3. What amount of bad debt expense would Summitt report on its April income statement under the two methods? Which amount better matches expense with revenue? Give your reason.

4. What amount of *net* accounts receivable would Summitt report on its April 30 balance sheet under the two methods? Which amount is more realistic? Give your reason.

Requirement 1

	General Journal				
DATE	ACCOUNT TITLES AND EXPLANATIONS	POST REF.	DEBIT	CREDIT	

Accounts Receivable   Bad Debt Expense

Requirement 2

General Journal

DATE		ACCOUNT TITLES AND EXPLANATIONS	POST REF.	DEBIT	CREDIT

Accounts Receivable

Allowance for Doubtful Accounts

Bad Debt Expense

Requirement 3

	Direct Write-Off Method	Allowance Method
Bad debt expense		

Requirement 4

	Direct Write-Off Method	Allowance Method
Accounts receivable		
Less: Allowance for doubtful accounts		
Accounts receivable, net		

Journal

DATE		ACCOUNT TITLES AND EXPLANATIONS	POST REF.	DEBIT	CREDIT

P9-6A ④ ⑤

Record the following selected transactions in the general journal of WM Gaming Supplies. Explanations are not required.

2019

Nov. 21   Received an $18,000, 60-day, 4 percent note from Barb Nuefield on account.

     30   Recorded VISA credit card sales of $26,000. VISA charges 3 percent of sales.

Dec. 31   Made an adjusting entry to accrue interest on the Nuefield note.

     31   Made an adjusting entry to record bad debt expense based on 3 percent of credit sales of $1,950,000.

     31   Made a compound closing entry for Interest Revenue and Bad Debt Expense (ignore credit card sales and charges).

2020

Jan. 20   Collected the maturity value of the Nuefield note.

Mar. 14   Lent $20,000 cash to Morgan Supplies, receiving a six-month, 5 percent note.

     30   Received a $5,600, 30-day, 10 percent note from Quin Carson on his past-due account receivable.

May 29   Carson dishonoured (failed to pay) his note at maturity; after attempting to collect his note for one month, wrote off the account as uncollectible.

Sep. 14   Collected the maturity value of the Morgan Supplies note.

     30   Wrote off as uncollectible the accounts receivable of Sue Parsons, $3,250 and Mac Gally, $5,200.

General Journal					
DATE		ACCOUNT TITLES AND EXPLANATIONS	POST REF.	DEBIT	CREDIT

Journal

DATE	ACCOUNT TITLES AND EXPLANATIONS	POST REF.	DEBIT	CREDIT

P9–9A ⑥

The comparative financial statements of Bita Company for 2020, 2019, and 2018 included the following selected data:

	2020	2019	2018
	(in thousands)		
Balance Sheet			
Current assets			
Cash	$ 80	$ 80	$ 40
Short-term investments	280	400	240
Receivables, net	760	600	480
Inventories	1,680	1,520	1,360
Prepaid expenses	120	120	80
Total current assets	$ 2,920	$ 2,720	$ 2,200
Total current liabilities	$ 1,920	$ 1,640	$ 1,520
Income Statement			
Sales revenue	$10,400	$10,000	$ 7,600

Required

1. Compute these ratios for 2020 and 2019, assuming that all sales are on account:

   a. Current ratio (round to two decimal places)

   b. Acid-test ratio (round to two decimal places)

   c. Days' sales in receivables (round to nearest full day)

   d. Accounts receivable turnover (round to nearest full turn)

2. Write a brief memo explaining to Adrian Crane, owner of Bita Company, which ratio values showed improvement from 2019 to 2020 and which ratio values deteriorated. Discuss whether this trend is favourable or unfavourable for the company.

Requirement 1

A. CURRENT RATIO: **2020**   **2019**

B. ACID-TEST RATIO:

C. DAYS' SALES IN AVERAGE RECEIVABLES: 2020   2019

D. ACCOUNTS RECEIVABLE TURNOVER:

Requirement 2

_____
_____
_____
_____
_____
_____
_____
_____
_____
_____
_____
_____
_____
_____
_____
_____
_____
_____
_____
_____
_____

*P9–10A Ⓐ1

A company received the following notes during 2020. The notes were discounted on the dates and at the rates indicated.

	A	B	C	D	E	F	G
1	**Note**	**Date**	**Principal Amount**	**Interest Rate**	**Term**	**Date Discounted**	**Discount Rate**
2	(a)	Jun. 15	$20,000	8%	60 days	Jul. 15	12%
3	(b)	Aug. 1	9,000	10	90 days	Aug. 27	12
4	(c)	Nov. 21	12,000	15	90 days	Dec. 4	15

Required Identify each note by letter, compute interest using a 365-day year for all notes, and round all interest amounts to the nearest cent. Explanations are not required.

1. Determine the due date and maturity value of each note.

2. Determine the discount and proceeds from the sale (discounting) of each note.

3. Write the general journal entry to record the discounting of note (b).

Requirement 1

NOTE	DUE DATE	PRINCIPAL + INTEREST		MATURITY VALUE
(a)	_____	_____	=	_____
(b)	_____	_____	=	_____
(c)	_____	_____	=	_____

Requirement 2

NOTE	MATURITY VALUE		DISCOUNT		PROCEEDS
(a)	_____	−	_____	=	_____
(b)	_____	−	_____	=	_____
(c)	_____	−	_____	=	_____

Requirement 3

General Journal					
DATE		ACCOUNT TITLES AND EXPLANATIONS	POST REF.	DEBIT	CREDIT

10 PROPERTY, PLANT, AND EQUIPMENT; AND GOODWILL AND INTANGIBLE ASSETS

LEARNING OBJECTIVES

1 Measure the cost of property, plant, and equipment.
2 Calculate and account for amortization.
3 Account for other issues: Amortization for income tax purposes, partial years, and revised assumptions.
4 Account for the disposal of property, plant, and equipment.
5 Account for natural resources.
6 Account for intangible assets and goodwill.
7 Describe the impact of IFRS on property, plant, and equipment, intangible assets, and goodwill.

SOME USEFUL TEXT INFORMATION (add your own notes too)

$$\text{Straight-line amortization} = \frac{\text{Cost} - \text{Residual value}}{\text{Useful life}}$$

$$\text{Units-of-production amortization per unit of output} = \frac{\text{Cost} - \text{Residual value}}{\text{Useful life in units of production}}$$

$$\text{DDB amortization} = \text{Asset book value} \times \text{DDB rate}$$

$$\text{Revised straight-line amortization} = \frac{\text{Cost} + \text{Betterments} - \text{Accumulated amortization} - \text{New residual value}}{\text{Estimated remaining useful life}}$$

- When disposing of PPE, always follow these three steps:
  1. Update amortization to date of sale, disposal, or trade.
  2. Calculate the gain or loss on disposal and report the gain or loss on the income statement.
  3. Remove the book balances from the asset account and its related accumulated amortization account.

1. $$\text{Amortization per unit of resource} = \frac{\text{Cost} - \text{Residual value}}{\text{Estimated total units of natural resource}}$$

2. $$\text{Amortization expense} = \text{Amortization per unit of resource} \times \text{Number of units of resource}$$

S10-6 ②

On January 1, 2020, FlyFast Airways purchased a used Bombardier jet at a cost of $50,000,000. FlyFast expects the plane to remain useful for five years (6,000,000 miles) and to have a residual value of $4,000,000. FlyFast expects the plane to be flown 750,000 miles the first year. (Note: "Miles" is the unit of measure used in the airline industry.)

1. Compute FlyFast's first-year amortization on the jet using the following methods:
   a. Straight-line   b. UOP   c. DDB
2. Show the jet's book value at the end of the first year under the straight-line method.

S10–8 ③

UpSky Airways purchased a small jet on January 1 at a cost of $40,000,000. UpSky expects the plane to remain useful for six years and to have a residual value of $4,000,000. UpSky is comparing the CCA method used for income tax purposes with the straight-line amortization method.

1. Calculate the amount of CCA, at a rate of 25 percent, that UpSky will be able to claim in its first year. Is this more or less than what it would show using the straight-line method?
2. Why does the Government of Canada, through the CCA, regulate the amount of amortization that a company can claim for income tax purposes?

_____

_____

_____

_____

_____

_____

_____

_____

_____

_____

_____

S10–11 ③

Red Pine Printers purchased equipment on January 1, 2016, for $250,000. The estimated residual value is $25,000, and the estimated useful life is 15 years. Red Pine Printers uses the straight-line method for amortization of its equipment. On January 1, 2019, Red Pine Printers revised the useful life to be 9 more years rather than 12. How much amortization would be recorded on December 31, 2019?

_____

_____

_____

_____

S10–12 ③

A fully amortized asset has a cost of $100,000 and zero residual value.

1. What is the asset's accumulated amortization? What is its carrying value?
2. The asset cost $100,000. Now suppose its residual value is $10,000. How much is its accumulated amortization if it is fully amortized?

_____

_____

_____

_____

S10-14 ④

A fully amortized asset has a cost of $100,000 and zero residual value.

1. What is the asset's accumulated amortization? What is its carrying value?
2. The asset cost $100,000. Now suppose its residual value is $10,000. How much is its accumulated amortization if it is fully amortized?

General Journal				
DATE	ACCOUNT TITLES AND EXPLANATIONS	POST REF.	DEBIT	CREDIT

S10-18 ⑥

Media-related companies have little in the way of property, plant, and equipment. Instead, their main asset is goodwill. When one media company buys another, goodwill is often the most costly asset acquired. Assume that Media Watch paid $800,000 on March 22 to acquire *The Thrifty Dime*, a weekly advertising paper. At the time of the acquisition, *The Thrifty Dime*'s balance sheet reported total assets of $1,300,000 and liabilities of $600,000. The fair market value of *The Thrifty Dime*'s assets was $1,200,000.

1. How much goodwill did Media Watch purchase as part of the acquisition of *The Thrifty Dime*?
2. Journalize Media Watch's acquisition of *The Thrifty Dime*.

General Journal				
DATE	ACCOUNT TITLES AND EXPLANATIONS	POST REF.	DEBIT	CREDIT

E10–2 ①

Phillipines Trucking bought three used trucks for $60,000. An independent appraisal of the trucks produced the following figures:

Truck	Appraised Value
1	$24,000
2	23,000
3	20,000

Phillipines Trucking paid $21,000 in cash and signed a note for the remainder. Record the purchase in the general journal on February 1, identifying each truck's individual cost in a separate Truck account. Phillipines Trucking rounds percentage calculations to two decimal places and all costs to the nearest whole dollar as it feels greater precision is not material.

General Journal

DATE		ACCOUNT TITLES AND EXPLANATIONS	POST REF.	DEBIT	CREDIT

E10–3 ①

Classify each of the following expenditures related to the cost of a machine:

	Cost or Betterment	Repair or Expense	Other
a. Purchase price			
b. Provincial sales tax paid on the purchase price			
c. Transportation and insurance while the machine is in transport from seller to buyer			
d. Installation			
e. Training of personnel for initial operation of the machine			
f. Special reinforcement to the machine platform			
g. Income tax paid on income earned from the sale of products manufactured by the machine			
h. Major overhaul to extend the machine's useful life by three years			
i. Ordinary recurring repairs to keep the machine in good working order			
j. Lubrication before the machine is placed in service			
k. Periodic lubrication after the machine is placed in service			
l. GST on the purchase price			

E10-5 ②

Crispy Fried Chicken bought equipment on January 2, 2018, for $33,000. The equipment was expected to remain in service for four years. At the end of the equipment's useful life, Crispy estimates that its residual value will be $6,000.

Prepare a schedule of *amortization expense, accumulated amortization,* and *book value* per year for the equipment under the straight-line method. Show your computations.

Straight-Line Amortization Schedule

DATE	ASSET COST	AMORTIZATION RATE	×	AMORTIZATION COST	=	AMORTIZATION EXPENSE	ACCUMULATED AMORTIZATION	ASSET BOOK VALUE

Amortization for the Year

E10-6 ②

My Porto Chicken bought equipment on January 2, 2018, for $33,000. The equipment was expected to remain in service for four years and to operate for 6,750 hours. At the end of the equipment's useful life, My Porto estimates that its residual value will be $6,000. The equipment operated for 675 hours the first year, 2,025 hours the second year, 2,700 hours the third year, and 1,350 hours the fourth year.

Prepare a schedule of *amortization expense, accumulated amortization,* and *book value* per year for the equipment under the units-of-production method. Show your computations.

Units-of-Production Amortization Schedule

	ASSET COST	AMORTIZATION PER ____	×	NUMBER OF ____	=	AMORTIZATION EXPENSE	ACCUMULATED AMORTIZATION	ASSET BOOK VALUE
DATE						Amortization for the Year		

E10–7 ②

Gigi's Baked Chicken bought equipment on January 2, 2018, for $33,000. The equipment was expected to remain in service for four years. At the end of the equipment's useful life, Gigi's estimates that its residual value will be $6,000.

Prepare a schedule of *amortization expense, accumulated amortization,* and *book value* per year for the equipment under the double-declining-balance method. Show your computations.

				Double-Declining-Balance Amortization Schedule		
				Amortization for the Year		
DATE	ASSET COST	DDB RATE	×	AMORTIZATION COST =	AMORTIZATION EXPENSE	ACCUMULATED AMORTIZATION	ASSET BOOK VALUE

Calculations:

E10–8 ②

On January 1, 2020, Murray Demolition, a Hamilton, Ontario, company specializing in blasting and removing buildings, purchased and took delivery of a new dump truck to add to its growing fleet. Murray Demolition has a high-class reputation and uses only the best and newest equipment on their worksites. The business spent $140,000 plus HST on the truck, which is expected to be useful to the business for four years, at which time it should be able to be sold for $60,000. Murray Demolition has always used the straight-line basis of calculating amortization. The new owners want to see the amortization schedules for the straight-line, UOP, and DDB methods just to be sure this makes sense. The business expects the truck to be useful for 200,000 kilometres—60,000 kilometres in Year 1, 50,000 kilometres in Year 4. Is there a problem with continuing to use the straight-line method?

Straight-Line Amortization Schedule

DATE	ASSET COST	AMORTIZATION RATE	×	AMORTIZATION COST	=	AMORTIZATION EXPENSE	ACCUMULATED AMORTIZATION	ASSET BOOK VALUE

Amortization for the Year

Units-of-Production Amortization Schedule

DATE	ASSET COST	AMORTIZATION PER ____	×	NUMBER OF ____	=	AMORTIZATION EXPENSE	ACCUMULATED AMORTIZATION	ASSET BOOK VALUE

Amortization for the Year

Double-Declining-Balance Amortization Schedule

Amortization for the Year

DATE	ASSET COST	DDB RATE ×	AMORTIZATION COST =	AMORTIZATION EXPENSE	ACCUMULATED AMORTIZATION	ASSET BOOK VALUE

Calculations:

E10-9 ②

Zhang Machine and Dye bought a machine on January 2, 2020, for $460,000. The machine was expected to remain in service for three years and produce 2,000,000 parts. At the end of its useful life, company officials estimated that, due to technological changes, the machine's residual value would only be $10,000. The machine produced 700,000 parts in the first year, 660,000 in the second year, and 650,000 in the third year.

Required

1. Prepare a schedule of *amortization expense* per year for the machine using the straight-line, UOP, and DDB amortization methods. Assume that in all cases the machine is valued at $10,000 at the end of the third year, and the third-year amortization is adjusted (set as a plug) to ensure this happens.

2. Which amortization method results in the highest net income in the second year? Does this higher net income mean the machine was used more efficiently under this method?

3. Which method tracks the wear and tear on the machine most closely? Why?

4. After one year under the DDB method, the company switched to the straight-line method. What is the new annual amortization expense amount?

Requirement 1

Amortization Expense Per Year			
YEAR	STRAIGHT-LINE	UNITS-OF-PRODUCTION	DOUBLE-DECLINING-BALANCE

Calculations:

Requirement 2

Requirement 3

Requirement 4

E10–12 ② ④

On January 13, 2019, Bill's Birdfeeders purchased store fixtures for $65,000 cash, expecting the fixtures to remain in service for 10 years. Bill's Birdfeeders has amortized the fixtures on a DDB basis with an estimated residual value of $5,000. On September 30, 2020, Bill's Birdfeeders sold the fixtures for $19,150 cash because they were not environmentally friendly. Record the amortization expense on the fixtures for the years ended December 31, 2019, and 2020, and the sale of the fixtures on September 30, 2020. Round all final amounts to the nearest dollar.

General Journal				
DATE	ACCOUNT TITLES AND EXPLANATIONS	POST REF.	DEBIT	CREDIT

Calculations:

E10-14 ① ② ④

Triad Freight is a large warehousing and distribution company that operates throughout Eastern Canada. Triad Freight uses the UOP method to amortize its trucks because its managers believe UOP amortization best measures the wear and tear on the trucks. Triad Freight trades in used trucks often to keep driver morale high and to maximize fuel efficiency. Consider these facts about one Mack truck in the company's fleet:

When acquired in 2016, the tractor/trailer rig cost $585,000 and was expected to remain in service for eight years, or 1,500,000 kilometres. Estimated residual value was $60,000. The truck was driven 150,000 kilometres in 2014, 195,000 kilometres in 2018, and 235,000 kilometres in 2019. After 100,000 kilometres in 2020, the company traded in the Mack truck for a Freightliner rig with a fair market value of $510,000 on August 15. Triad Freight paid cash of $40,000. This trade-in will bring in significantly more income to Triad Freight by reducing operating costs. Determine Triad Freight's cost of the new truck. Prepare the journal entry to record the trade-in.

Calculations:

General Journal

DATE		ACCOUNT TITLES AND EXPLANATIONS	POST REF.	DEBIT	CREDIT

E10–16 ③ ⑥

Biikman Company manufactures flat-screen monitors for the graphics industry. It purchased a patent for the design of a new monitor for $525,000. Although it gives legal protection for 20 years, the patent is expected to provide Biikman Company with a competitive advantage for only 10 years.

After using the patent for two years, Biikman Company learns at an industry trade show that another company is designing an even higher quality monitor. Based on this new information, Biikman Company decides to amortize the remaining cost of the patent over the year, giving the patent a total useful life of three years.

Required

1. Prepare the journal entry to record the purchase of the patent on January 1, 2020.
2. Assume straight-line amortization is used. Record the journal entry for amortization at December 31, 2020.
3. Record amortization for the year ended December 31, 2022.

Requirements 1 – 3

General Journal

DATE	ACCOUNT TITLES AND EXPLANATIONS	POST REF.	DEBIT	CREDIT

Calculations:

E10–21 ⑦

Note 1 of the notes to the financial statements (page 75) of the Loblaw 2016 Annual Report reads as follows:

> For the purpose of impairment testing, assets are grouped together into the smallest group of assets that generate cash inflows from continuing use that are largely independent of cash inflows of other assets or groups of assets. This grouping is referred to as a cash generating unit ("CGU"). The Company has determined that each location is a separate CGU for purposes of impairment testing.

Required

1. What is the "cash generating unit" for Loblaw?
2. What is *impairment testing*?

Requirements 1 & 2

_____

_____

_____

_____

_____

_____

_____

_____

_____

_____

_____

_____

_____

E10–22 ② ③ Serial Exercise

The Serial Exercise involves a company that will be revisited throughout relevant chapters in Volume 1 and Volume 2. You can complete the Serial Exercises using MyLab Accounting.

This exercise continues the Canyon Canoe Company situation from Chapter 9. Students do not have to complete prior exercises in order to answer this exercise.

Amber Wilson is continuing to review business practices. Currently, she is reviewing the company's property, plant, and equipment and has gathered the following information:

	A	B	C	D	E	F	G
1	Asset	Acquisition Date	Cost	Estimated Life	Estimated Residual Value	Amortization Method*	Monthly Amortization Expense
2	Canoes	Nov. 3, 2020	$ 4,800	4 years	$ 0	SL	$ 100
3	Land	Dec. 1, 2020	85,000			n/a	
4	Building	Dec. 1, 2020	35,000	5 years	5,000	SL	500
5	Canoes	Dec. 2, 2020	7,200	4 years	0	SL	150
6	Computer	Mar. 2, 2021	3,600	3 years	300	DDB	
7	Office Furniture	Mar. 3, 2021	3,000	5 years	600	SL	

*SL = Straight-line; DDB = Double-declining-balance

Required

1. Calculate the amount of monthly amortization expense for the computer and office furniture for 2020.

2. For each asset, determine the book value as of December 31, 2020. Then, calculate the amortization expense for the first six months of 2021 and the book value as of June 30, 2021.

3. Prepare a partial balance sheet showing Property, Plant, and Equipment as of June 30, 2021.

Requirement 1

Requirement 2

Asset	Cost	Monthly Amortization Expense	Months Amortized in 2020	Accumulated Amortization 12/31/20	Book Value 12/31/20
Canoes					
Land					
Building					
Canoes					
Totals					

Asset	Cost	Accum. Amort. 12/31/20	Book Value 12/31/20	Monthly Amort. Expense 2021	Months Amortized in 2021 (Jan. – Jun.)	Accum. Amort. 6/30/21	Book Value 6/30/21
Canoes							
Land							
Building							
Canoes							
Computer							
Office Furniture							
Totals							

Requirement 3

CANYON CANOE COMPANY			
Balance Sheet (partial)			
June 30, 2021			

P10-2A ②

On January 5, 2020, Paige Construction purchased a used crane at a total cost of $200,000. Before placing the crane in service, Paige spent $12,500 transporting it, $4,800 replacing parts, and $11,400 overhauling the engine. Karen Paige, the owner, estimates that the crane will remain in service for four years and have a residual value of $42,000. The crane's annual usage is expected to be 2,400 hours in each of the first three years and 2,200 hours in the fourth year. In trying to decide which amortization method to use, Mary Blundon, the accountant, requests an amortization schedule for each of the following generally accepted amortization methods: straight-line, UOP, and DDB.

Required

1. Assuming Paige Construction amortizes this crane individually, prepare an amortization schedule for each of the three amortization methods listed, showing asset cost, amortization expense, accumulated amortization, and asset book value. Assume a December 31 year-end. Round amortization per hour to four decimal places and the final answer to the nearest dollar.

2. Paige Construction prepares financial statements for its bankers using the amortization method that maximizes reported income in the early years of asset use. Identify the amortization method that meets the company's objective.

Calculations:

Requirement 1

Straight-Line Amortization Schedule

Amortization for the Year

DATE	ASSET COST	AMORTIZATION RATE	×	AMORTIZATION COST	=	AMORTIZATION EXPENSE	ACCUMULATED AMORTIZATION	ASSET BOOK VALUE

Units-of-Production Amortization Schedule

Amortization for the Year

DATE	ASSET COST	AMORTIZATION PER ____	×	NUMBER OF ____	=	AMORTIZATION EXPENSE	ACCUMULATED AMORTIZATION	ASSET BOOK VALUE

Requirement 1 (Continued)

Double-Declining-Balance Amortization Schedule

DATE	ASSET COST		DDB RATE		AMORTIZATION COST		AMORTIZATION EXPENSE		ACCUMULATED AMORTIZATION		ASSET BOOK VALUE
		×		=								

Amortization for the Year

Requirement 2

Calculations:

P10–3A ① ② ③

Digital Warehousing incurred the following costs in acquiring land and a building, making land improvements, and constructing and furnishing an office building for its own use:

a.	Purchase price of two hectares of land, including an old building that will be used for storage of maintenance equipment (land appraised market value is $1,300,000; building appraised market value is $300,000)	$1,150,000
b.	Real estate taxes in arrears on the land to be paid by Digital Warehousing	6,000
c.	Additional dirt and earth moving	6,000
d.	Legal fees on the land acquisition	4,500
e.	Fence around the boundary of the land	70,000
f.	Building permit for the office building	1,000
g.	Architect fee for the design of the office building	40,000
h.	Company signs near front and rear approaches to the company property	14,000
i.	Renovation of the storage building	150,000
j.	Concrete, wood, steel girders, and other materials used in the construction of the office building	700,000
k.	Masonry, carpentry, roofing, and other labour to construct the office building	550,000
l.	Parking lots and concrete walks on the property	31,500
m.	Lights for the parking lot, walkways, and company signs	12,500
n.	Salary of construction supervisor (90 percent to office building and 10 percent to storage building)	100,000
o.	Office furniture for the office building	125,000
p.	Transportation of furniture from seller to the office building	2,000

Digital Warehousing amortizes buildings over 40 years, land improvements over 20 years, and furniture over 6 years, all on a straight-line basis with zero residual value.

Required

1. Set up columns (or T-accounts) for Land, Land Improvements, Office Building, Storage Building, and Furniture. Show how to account for each of Digital's costs by listing the cost under the correct account. Determine the total cost of each asset.

2. Assuming that all construction was complete and the assets were placed in service on February 25, record amortization for the year ended December 31. Round figures to the nearest dollar.

Calculations:

Requirement 1

ITEM	LAND	LAND IMPROVEMENTS	OFFICE BUILDING	STORAGE BUILDING	FURNITURE

Calculations:

Requirement 2

General Journal

DATE		ACCOUNT TITLES AND EXPLANATIONS	POST REF.	DEBIT	CREDIT

Extra Journal Paper

DATE		ACCOUNTS TITLES AND EXPLANATIONS	POST REF.	DEBIT	CREDIT

P10–5A ① ② ③ ④

Assume that Rees Warehousing completed the following transactions:

2019

Mar. 3 Paid $8,000 cash for a used forklift.

5 Paid $1,500 to have the forklift engine overhauled.

7 Paid $1,000 to have the forklift modified for specialized moving of large flat-screen televisions.

Nov. 3 Paid $550 for an oil change and regular maintenance.

Dec. 31 Used the DDB method to record amortization on the forklift. (Assume a three-year life and no residual value.)

2020

Feb. 13 Replaced the forklift's broken fork for $400 cash, the deductible on Rees Warehousing's insurance. The new fork will not increase the useful life of the forklift.

Jul. 10 Traded in the forklift for a new forklift costing $18,000. The dealer granted a $3,000 allowance on the old forklift, and Rees Warehousing paid the balance in cash. Recorded 2020 amortization for the year to date and then recorded the exchange of forklifts. This transaction has commercial substance.

Dec. 31 Used the DDB method to record amortization on the new forklift. (Assume a five-year life and no residual value.)

Rees Warehousing's amortization policy indicates that the company will take a full month's amortization on purchases occurring up to and on the 15th day of the month and will not take any amortization for the month if the transaction occurs after the 15th day of the month.

Required Record the transactions in the general journal, indicating whether each transaction amount should be capitalized as an asset or expensed. Round all calculations to the nearest dollar.

General Journal

DATE		ACCOUNT TITLES AND EXPLANATIONS	POST REF.	DEBIT	CREDIT

General Journal

DATE	ACCOUNT TITLES AND EXPLANATIONS	POST REF.	DEBIT	CREDIT

Calculations:

P10–7A ⑤

Oilco Canada Limited sells refined petroleum products. The company's balance sheet includes reserves of oil assets.

Suppose Oilco paid $15 million cash for an oil lease that contained an estimated reserve of 1,990,000 barrels of oil. Assume that the company paid $550,000 for additional geological tests of the property and $170,000 to prepare the surface for drilling. Prior to production, the company signed a $120,000 note payable to have a building constructed on the property. Because the building provides onsite headquarters for the drilling effort and will be abandoned when the oil is depleted, its cost is debited to the Oil Properties account and included in amortization charges. During the first year of production, Oilco removed 125,000 barrels of oil, which it sold on credit for $75 per barrel.

Required

1. Make general journal entries to record all transactions related to the oil and gas property, including amortization and sale of the first-year production. Dates are not required.

2. Show the accounts and amounts that would be presented on the balance sheet.

Requirement 1

General Journal

DATE	ACCOUNT TITLES AND EXPLANATIONS	POST REF.	DEBIT	CREDIT

Requirement 1 (Continued)

		General Journal			
DATE		ACCOUNT TITLES AND EXPLANATIONS	POST REF.	DEBIT	CREDIT

Calculations:

Requirement 2

P10–8A ⑥

Part 1   WhiteWater West Industries is a waterpark construction company located in British Columbia. Assume that WhiteWater purchased another company that had the following totals on its financial statements:

Book value of assets..	$1,536,000
Market value of assets..	1,800,000
Liabilities..	540,000

Required

1. Make the general journal entry to record WhiteWater's purchase of the other company for $1,620,000 cash on April 3.
2. How should WhiteWater account for goodwill at year-end and in the future? Explain in detail.

Part 2   Suppose BlackBerry Ltd. purchased a patent for $1,400,000 on January 1. Before using the patent, BlackBerry incurred an additional cost of $250,000 for a lawsuit to defend the company's right to purchase it. Even though the patent gives BlackBerry legal protection for 20 years, company management has decided to amortize its cost over an 8-year period because of the industry's fast-changing technologies.

Required

1. Make general journal entries to record the patent transactions, including straight-line amortization for one year at December 31.
2. Show the accounts and amounts that would be presented on the balance sheet.

Part 1

Requirement 1

	General Journal			
DATE	ACCOUNT TITLES AND EXPLANATIONS	POST REF.	DEBIT	CREDIT

Requirement 2

_____
_____
_____
_____
_____

Part 2

Requirement 1

		General Journal			
DATE		ACCOUNT TITLES AND EXPLANATIONS	POST REF.	DEBIT	CREDIT

Requirement 2

Extra Journal Paper

DATE		ACCOUNTS TITLES AND EXPLANATIONS	POST REF.	DEBIT	CREDIT

11 CURRENT LIABILITIES AND PAYROLL

LEARNING OBJECTIVES

1 Account for current liabilities of a known amount.
2 Account for current liabilities that must be estimated.
3 Compute payroll amounts.
4 Record basic payroll transactions.
5 Report current liabilities on the balance sheet.
6 Describe the impact of IFRS on current liabilities.

SOME USEFUL TEXT INFORMATION (add your own notes too)

EXHIBIT 11–1 | Matching Objective: Putting Interest in the Correct Fiscal Year

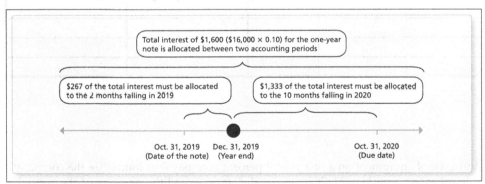

EXHIBIT 11–3 | Current Portion of Long-term Debt

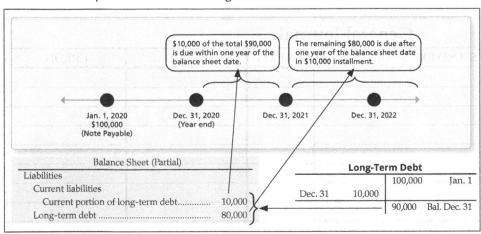

S11–3 ①

On July 10, Keller Company, a business located in Alberta, purchased $15,000 of inventory for resale on account. On July 25, Keller recorded the sale of that merchandise on account for $20,000 plus tax. On August 10, Keller remitted GST to the Receiver General. They had no other sales or input tax credits. Journalize all three transactions.

General Journal

DATE	ACCOUNT TITLES AND EXPLANATIONS	POST REF.	DEBIT	CREDIT

S11–6 ①

On December 31, 2019, Jabot purchased $16,000 of equipment on a one-year, 9 percent note payable. Journalize the company's purchase of equipment, the accrual of interest expense on May 31, 2020 (its fiscal year end), and the payment of the note plus interest on December 31, 2020.

General Journal

DATE	ACCOUNT TITLES AND EXPLANATIONS	POST REF.	DEBIT	CREDIT

General Journal

DATE		ACCOUNT TITLES AND EXPLANATIONS	POST REF.	DEBIT	CREDIT

S11-7 ②

Central Yard Equipment offers warranties on all its lawn mowers. It estimates warranty expense at 1.4 percent of sales. At the beginning of 2019, the Estimated Warranty Payable account had a credit balance of $2,200. During the year, Central Yard Equipment had $580,000 of sales and had to pay out $8,750 in warranty payments for repairs.

1. Prepare the required journal entries to record warranty expense and payments. Use December 31 for the journal entry date.
2. What is the balance of the warranty liability at the end of 2019? Indicate whether the balance is a debit or a credit.

Requirement 1

General Journal

DATE		ACCOUNT TITLES AND EXPLANATIONS	POST REF.	DEBIT	CREDIT

Requirement 2

Warranty Payable

S11–13 ③

Mike Klyn is paid $840 for a 40-hour workweek and time and a half for hours worked above 40.

1. Compute Klyn's gross pay for working 50 hours during the first week of February.
2. Klyn is single, and his income tax withholding is 20 percent of total pay. His only payroll deductions are taxes withheld, CPP of 4.95 percent, and EI of 1.66 percent. Compute Klyn's net pay for the week.

S11–14 ③

Return to the Mike Klyn payroll situation in S11–13. Klyn's employer, Jones Ski Corp., pays all the standard payroll expenses plus benefits for employee pensions (5 percent of gross pay), BC health insurance ($15 per employee per week), and disability insurance ($2 per employee per week). Assume February has four pay periods.

Compute Jones Ski Corp.'s total expense of employing Mike Klyn for the 50 hours that he worked during the first week of February. Show amounts to the nearest cent.

S11–16 (4)

After solving S11–13 and S11–14, journalize for Jones Ski Corp. the following expenses related to the employment of Mike Klyn on February 7:

a. Salary expense with payment to the employee

b. Benefits

c. Employer payroll expenses

Round all amounts to the nearest cent.

		General Journal			
DATE		ACCOUNT TITLES AND EXPLANATIONS	POST REF.	DEBIT	CREDIT

S11–17 (4)

After solving S11–13, S11–14, and S11–16, journalize for Jones Ski Corp. the remittance of this payroll to the CRA on March 15 (assuming that there was no additional payroll paid in February).

		General Journal			
DATE		ACCOUNT TITLES AND EXPLANATIONS	POST REF.	DEBIT	CREDIT

S11-18 (4)

Refer to the payroll information in S11–13, S11–14, and S11–16.

1. How much was the company's total payroll expense for the week for Mike Klyn?
2. How much cash did Mike Klyn take home for his work?
3. How much did the *employee* pay this week for
   a. Income tax?
   b. CPP and EI?
4. How much expense did the *employer* have this week for
   a. CPP and EI?
   b. Benefits?

_____

_____

_____

_____

_____

_____

_____

_____

_____

_____

_____

_____

_____

Under IFRS, what is the standard that must be met to report a contingent liability? Is it a higher or lower standard than under ASPE?

_____

_____

_____

_____

E11–2

Prepare the journal entries for Passport merchandisers, assuming that Passport merchandisers uses a perpetual inventory system. Passport merchandisers charges GST on all its sales at the rate of 5 percent and pays GST on all its purchases at the rate of 5 percent. Explanations are not required.

May	8	Purchased inventory, on account, FOB destination, from Seguin Wholesale, $2,000 plus applicable GST.
	10	Returned defective merchandise to Seguin, $300 plus applicable GST.
	12	Sold merchandise to Dainty Store on account for $3,000 plus applicable GST. Cost of the merchandise sold was $1,300.
	28	Collected balance on account from Dainty Store.
	30	Paid balance on account to Seguin.
Jun.	15	Prepare the remittance payment of GST based on only the above transactions in May.

General Journal				
DATE	ACCOUNT TITLES AND EXPLANATIONS	POST REF.	DEBIT	CREDIT

E11–4 ①

Make general journal entries to record the following transactions of Mehta Products for a two-month period:

Jun. 30   Recorded cash sales of $115,000 for the month plus PST of 8 percent collected on behalf of the province of Manitoba and GST of 5 percent. Record the two taxes in separate accounts.

Jul.   6   Sent June PST and GST to the appropriate authorities (Minister of Finance for PST and Receiver General for GST). Assume no GST input tax credits in this period.

	General Journal			
DATE	ACCOUNT TITLES AND EXPLANATIONS	POST REF.	DEBIT	CREDIT

E11–5 ①

Suppose Detweiler Technologies borrowed $2,000,000 on December 31, 2016, by issuing 4 percent long-term debt that must be paid in four equal annual instalments plus interest on the outstanding balance commencing January 2, 2018.

Required   Insert the appropriate amounts in the following excerpts from the company's partial balance sheet to show how Detweiler Technologies should report its current and long-term liabilities for this debt.

	December 31,			
	2017	2018	2019	2020
Current liabilities				
Current portion of long-term debt	$ _____	$ _____	$ _____	$ _____
Interest payable	$ _____	$ _____	$ _____	$ _____
Long-term liabilities				
Long-term debt	$ _____	$ _____	$ _____	$ _____

Calculations:

E11-14 ③

Sylvia Chan is a clerk in the shoe department of the Hudson's Bay store in Winnipeg. She earns a base monthly salary of $1,875 plus a 7 percent commission on her sales. Through payroll deductions, Chan donates $40 per month to a charitable organization and pays benefit premiums of $49.15. Compute Chan's gross pay and net pay for December, assuming her sales for the month are $50,000. The income tax rate on her earnings is 20 percent, the CPP contribution rate is 4.95 percent (account for the $3,500 basic annual exemption), and the EI premium rate is 1.66 percent. Chan has not yet reached the CPP or EI maximum earning levels.

E11-16 ③ ④

Brad Jackson works for a Bob's Burgers takeout for straight-time earnings of $15.25 per hour with time and a half for hours in excess of 35 per week. Jackson's payroll deductions include income tax of 21 percent, CPP of 4.95 percent on earnings (account for the $3,500 basic annual exemption), and EI of 1.66 percent on earnings. In addition, he contributes $10 per week to his Registered Retirement Savings Plan (RRSP). Assume Jackson worked 40 hours during the week. He has not yet reached the CPP or EI maximum earning levels.

Required

1. Compute Jackson's gross pay and net pay for the week.

2. Make a compound general journal entry for June 14 to record the restaurant's wage expense for Jackson's work, including his payroll deductions and the employer payroll costs. Round all amounts to the nearest cent. An explanation is not required. Remember, in a compound entry, all debits are entered first, then all credits. Check that total debits equals total credits.

Requirement 1

Requirement 2

General Journal

DATE		ACCOUNT TITLES AND EXPLANATIONS	POST REF.	DEBIT	CREDIT

E11–17 ③ ④

Twisted Indian Restaurant incurred salaries expense of $95,000 for September. The company's payroll expense includes CPP of 4.95 percent and EI of 1.4 times the employee payment, which is 1.66 percent of earnings. Also, the company provides the following benefits for employees: dental insurance (cost to the company of $5,723.09), life insurance (cost to the company of $441.09), and pension benefits through a private plan (cost to the company of $1,745.60). Record Twisted Indian Restaurant's payroll expenses for CPP, EI, and employee benefits on September 30. Ignore the CPP basic exemption.

\multicolumn{6}{c}{**General Journal**}
DATE		ACCOUNT TITLES AND EXPLANATIONS	POST REF.	DEBIT	CREDIT

EXHIBIT 11–10 | Employee Earnings Record for 2018

Employee Name and Address:

Jenkins, Jason C.

XX Camousen Crescent

Victoria, BC

Social Insurance No.: 111 111 111

Marital Status: Married

Net Claims Code: 4

Pay Rate: $700 per week; overtime $26.25 per hour

Job Title: Web Development Support

	A	B	C	D	E	F	G	H	I	J	K	L	M	N
1			Gross Pay				Deductions						Net Pay	
2	Week Ended	Hours	Straight Time	Overtime	Total	To Date	Federal Income Tax	Province of BC Income Tax	CPP	EI	United Way	Total	Amount	Cheque No.
3	Jan. 4	40	700.00		700.00	700.00	47.60	18.16	31.32	11.62	2.00	110.70	589.30	403
50	Dec. 3	40	700.00		700.00	35,437.50	47.60	18.16	31.32	11.62	2.00	110.70	589.30	1525
51	Dec. 10	40	700.00		700.00	36,137.50	47.60	18.16	31.32	11.62	2.00	110.70	589.30	1548
52	Dec. 17	44	700.00	105.00	805.00	36,942.50	62.28	25.27	36.52	13.36	2.00	139.43	665.57	1574
53	Dec. 24	48	700.00	210.00	910.00	37,852.50	81.48	32.99	41.71	15.11	2.00	173.29	736.71	1598
54	Dec. 31	46	700.00	157.50	857.50	38,710.00	70.47	29.13	39.11	14.24	2.00	154.95	702.55	1632
55	Total		36,400.00	2,310.00	38,710.00	38,710.00	2,798.16	1,082.28	1,742.90	642.59	104.00	6,369.93	32,340.07	

E11–18 ④

Study the Employee Earnings Record for Jason C. Jenkins in Exhibit 11–10. In addition to the amounts shown in the exhibit, the employer also paid all employee benefits plus (a) an amount equal to 5 percent of gross pay into Jenkins's pension retirement account, and (b) dental insurance for Jenkins at a cost of $35 per month and parking of $10 per month. Compute the employer's total payroll expense for employee Jason C. Jenkins during 2018. Carry all amounts to the nearest cent.

E11-19 ① ⑤

Assume Salem Electronics completed these selected transactions during December 2019:

1. Music For You Inc., a chain of music stores, ordered $105,000 worth of CD players. With its order, Music For You Inc. sent a cheque for $105,000. Salem Electronics will ship the goods on January 3, 2020.

2. The December payroll of $600,000 is subject to employee withheld income tax of 16 percent, CPP expenses of 4.95 percent for the employee and 4.95 percent for the employer, EI deductions of 1.66 percent for the employee and 1.4 times the employee rate of 1.66 percent for the employer. On December 31, Salem Electronics pays employees but accrues all tax amounts. Employees have not reached CPP or EI maximums.

3. Sales of $30,000,000 are subject to estimated warranty cost of 1 percent. This was the first year the company provided a warranty, and no warranty claims have been recorded or paid.

4. On December 2, Salem Electronics signed a $50,000 note payable that requires annual payments of $10,000 plus 5 percent interest on the unpaid balance each December 2. Salem calculates interest on this note based on days, not months.

Required   Report these liabilities on Salem Electronics' balance sheet at December 31, 2019. Round all amounts to the nearest dollar.

Calculations:

E11–20 ③ ④ Serial Exercise

The Serial Exercise involves a company that will be revisited throughout relevant chapters in Volume 1 and Volume 2. You can complete the Serial Exercises using MyLab Accounting.

This exercise continues recordkeeping for the Canyon Canoe Company. Students do not have to complete prior exercises in order to answer this question.

On January 1, Amber Wilson hired a part-time employee to work in the rental booth. The employee is paid $2,000 monthly. The following additional payroll information is available for the January 31, 2021, pay date:

Federal income tax to be withheld	$138.55
Provincial income tax to be withheld	99.70
CPP	84.56
EI	33.20

Required

1. Compute the rental-booth employee's gross pay and net pay for the month.
2. Make one general journal entry to record Canyon Canoe Company's salary expense for the rental-booth employee, including the payroll deductions and the employer payroll costs. Round all amounts to the nearest cent.

Requirement 1

Requirement 2

General Journal

DATE		ACCOUNT TITLES AND EXPLANATIONS	POST REF.	DEBIT	CREDIT

P11–1A ① ②

The following selected transactions of Golden Bear Construction occurred during 2019 and 2020. The company's year end is December 31.

2019

Jan.	3	Purchased a machine at a cost of $350,000 plus 5 percent GST, signing a 5 percent, 180-day note payable for that amount.
	29	Recorded the month's sales of $1,570,000 (excludes PST and GST), 80 percent on credit and 20 percent for cash. Sales amounts are subject to 8 percent PST and 5 percent GST.
Feb.	5	Paid January's PST and GST to the appropriate authorities.
	28	Borrowed $3,000,000 on a 3 percent note payable that calls for annual instalment payments of $300,000 principal plus interest.
Jul.	3	Paid the six-month, 5 percent note at maturity.
Nov.	30	Purchased inventory for $150,000 plus GST, signing a six-month, 5 percent note payable.
Dec.	31	Accrued warranty expense, which is estimated at 2 percent of annual sales of $8,000,000.
	31	Accrued interest on all outstanding notes payable. Make a separate interest accrual entry for each note payable.

2020

Feb.	28	Paid the first instalment and interest for one year on the long-term note payable.
May	31	Paid off the 5 percent note plus interest at maturity.

Required Record the transactions in the company's general journal. Use days in any interest accrual calculations, not months. Round all amounts to the nearest whole dollar. Explanations are not required.

General Journal					
DATE		ACCOUNT TITLES AND EXPLANATIONS	POST REF.	DEBIT	CREDIT

General Journal

DATE		ACCOUNT TITLES AND EXPLANATIONS	POST REF.	DEBIT	CREDIT

P11–3A ③

The partial monthly records of Westwood Golf Shop show the figures below.

Required

1. Determine missing amounts a, b, c, and d.
2. Prepare the general journal entry to record Westwood Golf Shop's payroll on August 31. Credit Payroll Payable for net pay. No explanation is required.

Requirement 1

SUPPLY MISSING PAYROLL AMOUNTS

Employee Earnings

Regular employee earnings	$19,947	Medical insurance	$ 541
Overtime pay	a	Total deductions	7,947
Total employee earnings	b	Net pay	17,595

Deductions and Net Pay

Accounts Debited

Withheld income tax	6,379	Salaries Expense	d
Canada Pension Plan	c	Wages Expense	6,938
Employment Insurance	478	Sales Commission Expense	1,681

Requirement 2

General Journal

DATE		ACCOUNT TITLES AND EXPLANATIONS	POST REF.	DEBIT	CREDIT

Calculations:

P11-4A ③ ④

Assume that Raji Patel is a vice-president in Maple Capital's leasing operations. During 2018 she worked for the company all year at a $7,500 monthly salary. She also earned a year-end bonus equal to 10 percent of her salary.

Patel's federal income tax withheld during 2018 was $2,398 per month. Also, there was a one-time federal withholding tax of $4,512 on her bonus cheque. She paid $356.85 per month into the CPP until she had paid the maximum of $2,593.80. In addition, Patel paid $157.50 per month EI through her employer until the maximum of $858.22 had been reached. She had authorized Maple Capital to make the following payroll deductions: RRSP contribution of $55 per month and United Way donation of $37.50 per month.

Maple Capital incurred CPP expense equal to the amount deducted from Patel's pay and EI expense equal to 1.4 times the amount Patel paid. In addition, Maple Capital paid dental and drug insurance of $38 per month and pension benefits of 7 percent of her base salary.

Required

1. Compute Patel's gross pay, payroll deductions, and net pay for the full year 2018. Round all amounts to the nearest cent.

2. Compute Maple Capital's total 2018 payroll expense for Patel.

3. Prepare Maple Capital's general journal entries at December 31 (explanations are not required) to record its expense for the following:

   a. Patel's total earnings for the year, her payroll deductions, and her net pay. Debit Salary Expense and Bonus Expense as appropriate for salary and bonus. Credit liability accounts for the payroll deductions and Cash for net pay.

   b. Employer payroll expenses for Patel. Credit the appropriate liability accounts.

   c. Benefits provided to Patel. Credit Health Insurance Payable and Company Pension Payable.

Requirement 1

Requirement 2

Requirement 3

General Journal

DATE		ACCOUNT TITLES AND EXPLANATIONS	POST REF.	DEBIT	CREDIT

P11–5A ③ ④

The payroll records of Radii Video Productions Inc. provide the following information for the weekly pay period ended September 21:

	A	B	C	D	E	F	G	H
1	Employee	Hours Worked	Hourly Earnings Rate	Income Tax	Canada Pension Plan	Employment Insurance	United Way	Year-to-Date Earnings at End of Previous Week
2	Molly Dodge	43	$ 30	$474.10	$ 0.00	$ 0	$25	$61,500
3	Tally Allard	40	17.75	170.40	35.15	11.79	2	19,760
4	George Tanaka	49	15	192.60	39.72	13.32	2	20,250
5	Luigi Valenti	42	20	240.80	0.00	0	5	58,950

Tally Allard and George Tanaka work in the office, and Molly Dodge and Luigi Valenti work in sales. All employees are paid time and a half for hours worked in excess of 40 hours per week. Assume that the company contributes an amount equal to 8 percent of each employee's gross pay to a retirement program. Each employee also accrues 4 percent vacation pay based on the gross pay. Show computations.

Required

1. Enter the appropriate information in a payroll register.
2. Record the payroll information in the general journal, crediting net pay to Cash.
3. The employer's payroll costs include matching each employee's CPP contribution and paying 1.4 times the employees' EI premium. Record the employer's payroll costs in the general journal.
4. Why was there no deduction of CPP or EI for Dodge and no deduction of EI for Valenti?
5. What would be the vacation pay liability for Radii Video Productions Inc.?

Requirement 1

PAYROLL REGISTER						
		GROSS PAY				
EMPLOYEE NAME	HRS.	STRAIGHT TIME	OVERTIME	TOTAL	INCOME TAX	CANADA PENSION PLAN

Calculations:

Requirement 1 (Continued)

PAYROLL REGISTER								
DEDUCTIONS			NET PAY		ACCOUNT DEBITED			
EMPLOYMENT INSURANCE	UNITED WAY	TOTAL	AMOUNT	CHQ. NO.	RETIREMENT PROGRAM	OFFICE SALARIES EXPENSE	SALES SALARIES EXPENSE	

Requirements 2 & 3

\ General Journal				
DATE	ACCOUNT TITLES AND EXPLANATIONS	POST REF.	DEBIT	CREDIT

Requirements 4 & 5

Extra Journal Page

DATE		ACCOUNTS TITLES AND EXPLANATIONS	POST REF.	DEBIT	CREDIT

P 11–9A ① ② ⑤

Pontoon Creations produces and sells customized boats for resorts in Ontario. The company offers a 60-day, all parts and labour—and an extra 90-day, parts-only—warranty on all of its products. The company had the following transactions in 2020:

Jan. 31 Sales for the month totalled $80,000 (not including HST), of which 90 percent were on credit. The company collects 13 percent HST on all sales and estimates its warranty costs at 4 percent of sales.

31 Based on last year's property tax assessment, the company estimated that the property taxes for the year would be $60,000 (3 percent of last year's $2,000,000 assessed value). Recorded the estimated property taxes for the month; credited Property Taxes Payable.

Feb. 4 Completed repair work for a customer. The parts ($500) and labour ($850) were all covered under the warranty. Record the labour as Wages Expense.

7 Sent a cheque for the appropriate HST for the month of January (the company had paid $3,700 of HST on purchases in January).

28 Recorded the estimated property taxes for the month of February.

28 Sales for the month totalled $92,000 (not including HST), of which 85 percent were on credit. The company estimates its warranty costs at 4 percent of sales.

Mar. 7 Sent a cheque for the appropriate HST amount for the month of February (the company had paid $4,750 of HST on purchases in February).

8 Pontoon Creations received notice that it was being sued by a customer for an accident resulting from the breakdown of its product. The company's lawyer was reluctant to estimate the likely outcome of the lawsuit, but another customer indicated that a similar case had resulted in a $500,000 settlement.

15 Completed repair work for a customer. The parts ($2,500) and labour ($1,200) were all covered under the warranty.

21 Completed repair work for a customer. The parts ($750) were covered by the warranty, but the labour ($500) was not. Payment from the customer is due for the labour in 30 days.

31 Sales for the month totalled $88,000 (not including HST), of which 90 percent were on credit. The company estimates its warranty costs at 4 percent of sales.

31 Received the property tax assessment for 2020. It showed the assessed value of the property to be $2,200,000 and a tax rate of 3 percent of the assessed value. The company made the appropriate adjustment to the Property Taxes Payable account. Property tax will be paid on December 31, 2020.

Required

1. Journalize the above transactions.

2. Show the appropriate financial statement presentation for all liabilities at March 31, 2020.

Requirement 1

		General Journal			
DATE		ACCOUNT TITLES AND EXPLANATIONS	POST REF.	DEBIT	CREDIT

Requirement 1 (Continued)

General Journal					
DATE		ACCOUNT TITLES AND EXPLANATIONS	POST REF.	DEBIT	CREDIT

Requirement 2

Extra Statement Paper

Extra Statement Paper

Extra Statement Paper

Extra Journal Page

DATE		ACCOUNT TITLES AND EXPLANATIONS	POST REF.	DEBIT	CREDIT

Extra Journal Page

DATE		ACCOUNT TITLES AND EXPLANATIONS	POST REF.	DEBIT	CREDIT

Extra Journal Page

DATE		ACCOUNT TITLES AND EXPLANATIONS	POST REF.	DEBIT	CREDIT

Extra Balance Sheet – Report Format

Extra Balance Sheet – Report Format

Extra Balance Sheet – Report Format

Extra Balance Sheet – Report Format